The Journey
to Discover
GOD

The Holy Spirit Takes
the Christian Life to Another Level

by D. Michael Cotten

©2019, D Michael Cotten
All Rights Reserved
ISBN: 978-1-936497-39-3
Contact the Author at
dmichaelcotten@att.net

Searchlight Press
Who are you looking for?
Publishers of thoughtful Christian books since 1994.
PO Box 554
Henderson, TX 75653-0554
214.662.5494
info@Searchlight-Press.com
www.Searchlight-Press.com

TABLE OF CONTENTS

INTRODUCTION

Premise for this book;
Everything needed for life and GODliness
has been provided.

Jesus did not die for your sins to give you a way to Heaven, Jesus died for your sins and was raised from the dead to give Believers right standing with GOD, so that Jesus could send His Spirit to be in and on Believers. Jesus Christ was one man on Earth, but through the Holy Spirit can have a personal relationship with every Believer, who ask to be baptized with the Holy Spirit. Jesus did not start his ministry, nor do a single miracle, until Jesus was baptized with the Holy Spirit, at His baptism. All the promises of GOD are thousands of years old and require Believers to find and appropriate the promises by faith or belief in the finished works of GOD. The Holy Spirit will guide Believers, who ask direction, to live the life GOD made for you while you are on earth.

GOD's creation of the world and its future has been set in motion by GOD. Jesus Christ has fully reconciled mankind to GOD. GOD can now send the Holy Spirit to Believers, who ask for the Holy Spirit, in the same way that GOD sent the Holy Spirit to be in and on Jesus Christ at His Baptism.

At Creation: GOD made

all the air mankind would ever need to breathe,

all the water mankind would ever need to drink,

all the food sources mankind would ever need for nourishment,

all the majesty of the mountains and oceans mankind would ever need for art,

all the beauty of the heavens, the stars, and the sun, that

mankind would ever need for enjoyment of life.

At redemption: Jesus Christ made all, the promises of GOD available for mankind to motivate their life,

> at redemption Jesus Christ made right-standing with GOD available to all mankind,
>
> at redemption Jesus Christ redeemed mankind from all the curses,
>
> at redemption Jesus Christ bore our griefs and carried our sorrows,
>
> at redemption Jesus Christ paid for our transgressions and absolved our iniquities,
>
> at redemption Jesus Christ was berated to deliver peace to mankind,
>
> at redemption Jesus Christ body was scourged for the healing of mankind's body,
>
> at the redemption of Jesus Christ, the travail of His soul justified mankind for all who choose GOD.

All the gifts of GOD Almighty and Jesus Christ, including the Holy Spirit, are finished and the Believer owns "the finished works of Jesus Christ and GOD Almighty". Believers reaching in to the Spiritual world of ages past and appropriating something that is outside time is a difficult concept. This book will teach new concepts from scripture to illuminate GOD's foundational principals and the Believer's authority restored with the Holy Spirit and the study of the function of the mind and brain as it relates to Christianity.

Believers should not be stymied living in the era of Jesus Christ "under the law" but live with the Holy Spirit under the New Covenant given Believers by Jesus Christ. The new era of the Holy Spirit with the power that raised Jesus from the dead is inside every Believer, who has a relationship with the Holy Spirit. Welcome to the journey to find and know GOD, the Holy

Spirit.

Words from the Author about Writing Style

This book is not written in strict adherence to grammatical rules. The Bible and concepts of GOD are complicated. To unpack the compound sentences and the interaction of the visible and invisible world; each page will contain highlights, capital letters, quotes, underlines and cascading verses, to add sound and definition to the words.

FOUNDATIONAL TRUTH

Before we start, here is a synopsis of four foundational truths to help understand the construction and timing of the Bible; these truths are expounded later.

• At the time, of the Lord's death and resurrection, **all of mankind's names were written in the, "Lamb's book of Life". Therefore, there is a lifeline available for every human to accept the cancellation of sin.** The only way for any name to be removed from the "Lamb's book of Life" is to be blotted out for rejecting Jesus Christ as Savior and living unto yourself as your god.

• **The power of sin is death;** sin is **choosing to live unto yourself,** and not living in covenant with GOD, **which is idolatry.** The new covenant with GOD and redemption from Jesus Christ is eternal life and the presence of GOD inside Believers in the third person of the Trinity, the Holy Spirit. **If you believe in Jesus Christ and live unto Him, death has no power over you** because there is no sin in your life, Jesus fulfilled the law and your sin and your lawlessness is not counted against you.

• Believers must speak to, listen to, and follow GOD's lead to have the abundant life given by Jesus Christ. Believers must be going in the same direction as their GOD, every day. To be going in the same direction as your GOD you must communicate with GOD, daily, and minute by minute, capturing every moment. Believers not confirming the direction for their actions with the Holy Spirit, will not know the will of GOD for their next issue of life.

• Everyone has heard the account of Adam and Eve eating from the tree of the knowledge of good and evil; what happened to mankind when they knew the essence of good and evil? **GOD did not tell Adam and Eve they were naked,** their conscience was activated, and they knew they had transgressed their innate moral code and they were afraid and ashamed, and Adam and Eve hid from GOD's presence. Until this moment, in the Garden of Eden, there was no consciousness of transgression, because no human had acted against the word of GOD.

Mankind's Spirit was created from a part of GOD. GOD created, the Heavens and the earth, followed by light and water and GOD made all living things out of the building blocks GOD created, (soil and sea) with the one exception of Mankind's Spirit which GOD made from part of Himself.

For example, at Creation;

Out of the earth, GOD spoke to the earth to bring forth grass and seed-bearing plants, herbs and trees. These plants were made from the earth, sustained by the earth and return to the earth.

Out of the seas, GOD spoke to the seas to bring forth fish and whales and out of the seas were the sea creatures sustained and at death the sea creatures return to the seas.

Out of the earth, GOD spoke to the earth to bring forth animals, the animals were sustained by the earth and at their death they return to the earth.

Out of the earth, GOD made man's body, man's body is sustained by the earth, and at death mankind's body is returned to the earth.

Take notice:

Out of GOD, GOD created Man's Spirit from part of Himself, GOD sustains Man's Spirit, and Man's Spirit will return to GOD for judgment: eternal life or eternal damnation.

Consider the Biblical timing; **GOD created** the Spirit of man in Genesis 1:27

Genesis 1:27 So God created man in his own image, in the image of God he created him; male and female he created them.

Significantly later, In the next chapter of Genesis; GOD made mankind's body. **GOD made man's body** from the dust of the earth and breathed GOD's Spirit into Adam in Genesis 2:7.

> Gen 2:7 then **the LORD God formed the man of dust** from the ground and breathed into his nostrils the breath of life, and the man became a living creature.

The Foundational truth is; the Believer's Spirit is created out of GOD, Himself, and GOD sustains His creation and the Spirit of all mankind will return to GOD for judgment: eternal life with GOD or eternal separation from GOD. No other Earthly creature will be blessed with eternal life with GOD.

Every name of every person, who ever lived or will live, is written in the "Lamb's book of Life", this fact reveals the love expressed, for Mankind, by Jesus Christ. The scripture says that Jesus died once, for all of mankind, and reconciled mankind to GOD; those who believed in the past or will believe in the future. The Apostles Paul and John inform us that **at the time of the resurrection of Jesus Christ every person's name in the world, from the beginning of time to the end of time was written in the "Lamb's Book of Life".**

> **Jesus died for all, as payment, for the universe of sin; sin is unbelief in your need for a Savior and GOD.** Lawlessness is bad behavior, but not believing in your need for GOD in your life, is the sin unto death. The "Lamb's book of Life" includes all the people who lived before Jesus went to the cross and all the people who lived and will live after the cross; including the good people and the bad people.

> > 2nd Corinthians 5:14 For the love of Christ constraineth us; because we thus judge, that if **one died for all**, then were all dead: And that **he died for all**, that they which live **should not henceforth live unto themselves**, but unto him which died for them, and rose again and he died for all, **that those who live might no longer live for themselves** but for him (Jesus Christ) who for their sake died and was raised.

The names in the "Lamb's book of Life" **are not** added as people become Christians but were established when Jesus Christ paid the penalty for the universe of sin and the elimination of the law requiring judgment for the motivation for a sinful life. If anyone

chooses to live unto themselves and not to live unto Jesus Christ, who died and was raised again for the sin of the world, their name will be blotted out of the, "Lamb's book of Life".

At the White Throne Judgment, the names of **unbelievers** will be **blotted out** of the, "Lamb's Book of Life". Jesus has paid the price for every person who ever lived to be saved; will you receive His love?

> If mankind does not accept salvation, through Jesus Christ, and exchange the motivation for a life of sin for right standing with GOD, **their name will be blotted out of the Lamb's Book of Life.**
>
> Listen to the Lord in Revelation 3:5 He that overcometh, the same shall be clothed in white raiment; and **I will not** blot out his name out of the book of life, but I will confess his name before my Father, and before his angels.

Jesus died that all could have the total wellbeing of salvation but not all will receive salvation and not all will be healed or delivered, but all had the opportunity to believe and receive.

FOUNDATIONAL TRUTH THREE

**The New Covenant is between
Jesus Christ and GOD Almighty and begins
the era of the Holy Spirit.**

The New Covenant for Christians is **not** between GOD and mankind and not between GOD and Believers but **is between Father GOD and Jesus Christ.** Christians have inherited, at the death of Jesus Christ, the benefits of the covenant between GOD and Jesus Christ. GOD made a covenant with Adam and Eve and Adam and Eve broke the covenant with GOD. GOD made a covenant with Israel and Israel broke the covenant with GOD. **So, Father GOD made a covenant with Jesus and Jesus was faithful and fulfilled the law and was sacrificed for the universe of sin and Jesus absorbed the punishment. The Lord's sacrifice paid for the sins of the world from the beginning of time to the end of time, fulfilling His covenant with GOD. Jesus left his estate to Believers with the Holy Spirit as executor.**

The New Covenant does not depend on man's faithfulness but is completely based on GOD's faithfulness. The gospels are written about the activities of Jesus during **the old covenant** between GOD and Israel. If Jesus **had not** gone to the cross to satisfy the requirements of the old covenant and bring forth the New Covenant; mankind would die in their sin.

The ascension of Jesus to Heaven marks the beginning of the New Covenant between GOD and Jesus Christ, not mankind and GOD. Believers in Jesus Christ, as Savior, are the beneficiary of the Covenant between GOD and Jesus. **Think of the Holy Spirit as the executor of the inheritance of Jesus Christ and if invited the Holy Spirit will abide with Believers to explain**

the inheritance and tell you of things to come. The most significant part of the Lords estate inherited by Believers is the gift of the Holy Spirit to be inside every Believer who asks GOD for the Holy Spirit.

Life with the Holy Spirit of Jesus Christ is the next era of GOD with mankind, "the New Covenant" is **GOD inside Believers.** Listen to these verses as the Apostle Paul introduces the new covenant life with the Spirit of Jesus Christ living inside Believers and Believers living through leadership from the Holy Spirit. Study the New Testament to understand about the Holy Spirit of Jesus Christ.

Listen to the Apostle Paul;

Galatians 2:20 <u>So I am not the one living now</u> **it is Christ living in me.** I still live in my body, but I live by faith in the Son of God. He is the one who loved me and gave himself to save me.

2nd Timothy 2:11 The saying is trustworthy, for: **If we have died with him, we will also live with him**; if we endure, we will also reign with him; if we deny him, he also will deny us; if we are faithless, **he remains faithful**— <u>for he cannot deny himself.</u>

Philippians 3:9 and **be found in him,** not having a righteousness of my own that comes from the law, but righteousness which comes through **faith in Christ, the righteousness from God that depends on faith**—that <u>I may know him and the power of his resurrection,</u> and may share his sufferings, becoming like him in his death, that by any means possible I may attain the resurrection from the dead.

1st Corinthians 6:17 But he who is joined to the Lord **becomes one spirit with him.**

Almighty GOD is one GOD in three persons, if Believers have the Holy Spirit living inside you, **then Believers have the GOD of Creation, Jesus Christ, the Redeemer, and the Holy Spirit living inside Believers**.

The Foundational Truth is that Jesus died **to give Believers the Holy Spirit** and start a one-on-one relationship with Believers. Galatians 4:4 Butwhen the fullness of time had come, God sent forth his Son, <u>born of woman</u>, <u>born under the law</u>, **to redeem those who were under the law**, so that we might receive adoption as sons. And because you are sons, **God has sent the Spirit of his Son into our hearts**, crying, "Abba! Father!" So you are no longer a slave, but a son, and if **a son, then an heir through God.**

What does this truth mean to **Believers: Believers can call on the standing of Jesus Christ in every situation in their life, because Believers are heirs through GOD!**
> Believers can operate in the standing of the sinless life of Jesus Christ for the salvation of your life. 2nd Corinthians 5:14
> Believers can stand in the standing of Jesus Christ against the curses of the law from Deuteronomy 28:15-68.
> Believers can be confident in the standing of Jesus Christ authority to reconcile mankind to GOD. 2nd Corinthians 5:19-21
> Believers can rest in the standing of Jesus Christ and Father GOD's love for the world. John 3:14-18

The Believer accessing the standing of Jesus Christ, to complete an act of kindness will be successful. The Holy Spirit brings all the attributes of Jesus Christ with Him to abide with Believers; salvation, redemption, deliverance, healing, love, and peace.

When Christ is living inside you, your standing is not natural, but it is super-natural.

Conscience and condemnation

Everyone has heard the account of Adam and Eve, eating from the tree of the knowledge of good and evil; what happened to mankind when they knew the essence of good and evil? What does the scripture say? Instantly after breaking covenant with GOD, Adam and Eve knew they were naked and were ashamed and feared seeing GOD, so they were condemned by their conscience and hid. **GOD did not tell Adam and Eve they were naked,** their conscience was activated, and they knew they had transgressed their innate moral code and they were afraid and ashamed, and Adam and Eve hid from GOD's presence. Until this moment in the Garden of Eden, there was no consciousness of transgression, because no human had acted against the word of GOD. This first choice of mankind to reject covenant with GOD and live unto themselves changed the management of their mind, added chaos to their brain, and added death and deterioration to their life (possibly changed their DNA). Death and deterioration came through disobedience.

GOD did not create mankind's body to die nor the mind to be filled with stress. The first sign of the change in the bodies of Adam and Eve was being conscious of breaking God's word and shame of the knowledge of their nakedness and fear in their heart at the sound of GOD's voice. **It is the conscience that condemns mankind and the conscience of dead works that must be purged through the blood of our Savior for salvation.** Listen to the creation of the New Covenant and the purging of the conscience of Believers, to reverse the effects of the sin of Adam and Eve.

> Hebrews 8:6 But as it is, <u>Christ has obtained a ministry that is as much more excellent than the old as the covenant he mediates is better, since it is enacted on</u>

better promises. For if that first covenant had been faultless, then should no place have been sought for the second. For finding fault with them, he saith, Behold, the days come, saith the Lord, when **I will** make a new covenant with the house of Israel **and with the house of Judah:** Not according to the covenant that I made with their fathers in the day when I took them by the hand to lead them out of the land of Egypt; because they continued not in my covenant, and I regarded them not, saith the Lord. For this is the covenant that **I will** make with the house of Israel after those days, saith the Lord; **I will** put my laws into their mind, and write them in their hearts: and **I will** be to them a God, and they shall be to me a people:... Heb 8:12 **For I will be merciful toward their iniquities, and I will remember their sins no more."**
Ephesians 1:7 In whom we have redemption through his blood, the forgiveness of sins, according to the riches of his grace; Wherein he hath abounded toward us in all wisdom and prudence;

Hebrews announces that the old Covenant is inadequate and that there must be a new Covenant comparing it to the Temple and the separation of the sanctuary from the Holy of Holies by a large curtain which at the death of Jesus Christ was torn from top to bottom to forever allow Believers to enter the presence of GOD Almighty and to be with GOD, right now.

Hebrews 9:8 By this the Holy Spirit indicates that the way into the holy places is not yet opened as long as the first section is still standing (which is symbolic for the present age). According to this arrangement, gifts **and sacrifices are offered that cannot perfect the conscience of the worshiper**.

Now the announcement of Christ sacrifice and victory.

> Hebrews 9:11 **But when Christ appeared as a high priest of the good things that have come**, then through the greater and more perfect tent (not made with hands, that is, not of this creation) he (Jesus) entered once for all into the holy places, not by means of the blood of goats and calves but by means of his own blood, **thus securing an eternal redemption**.

It is this new relationship with Jesus Christ that offers the perfection of the Believer's conscience, through His blood and therefore the ability to put on the New Creation life and **seal your new Spirit with the Holy Spirit free of all condemnation and reversing the sin of Adam and Eve.**

> Hebrews 9:14 how much more will the blood of Christ, who through the eternal Spirit offered himself without blemish to God, **purify our conscience from dead works to serve the living God.**

How do Believers respond if your conscience condemns you? Believers must reassure our heart with the word and the love we have from our GOD.

> 1st John 3:18 My children, our love should not be just words and talk; **it must be true love,** which shows itself in action. This, then, is how we will know that we belong to the truth; this is how we will be confident in God's presence. **If our conscience condemns us, we know that God is greater than our conscience and that he knows everything.** And so, my dear friends, if our conscience does not condemn us, we have courage in **God's presence**. We receive from him whatever we ask, because we obey his commands and do what pleases him. **What he commands is that we believe in his Son Jesus Christ and love one another, just as**

Christ commanded us. Those who obey God's commands live in union with God and God lives in union with them. **And because of "the Spirit" that God has given (Believers) us we know that God lives in union with (Believers) us**. Good News Bible

The Believer's Spirit is alive and redeemed from the sin of Adam and Eve and your conscience has been sprinkled with the sinless blood of Jesus Christ.

THE JOURNEY
TO DISCOVER
GOD.

CHAPTER 1

A Believer can "only" access by faith,
what Jesus has made available through His grace.

The world's greatest love story; Abraham and Sarah were promised a son that would be a blessing to the world. After many years GOD's promise came to life as a son named Isaac. As their son Isaac was maturing, GOD told Abraham to sacrifice his only son, whom Abraham loved. Abraham took his son and committed to sacrificing his son, whom he loved, because he loved GOD. As he was about to kill Isaac the angel stopped him and GOD said **Now, I know that you love me,** because you did not withhold your son from Me, the son whom you loved.

> **Now the world can say to GOD Almighty, I know that GOD loves me, because GOD did not withhold His son Jesus from me, the Son He loves.**

The Bible reveals GOD's love for mankind in every chapter and verse. Listen to Isaiah continue to describe the love GOD has for Mankind;

> **Isaiah 9:6** For to us a child is born, to us **a son is given;** and the government shall be upon his shoulder, and his name shall be called Wonderful Counselor, Mighty God, Everlasting Father, Prince of Peace. Of the increase of his government and of peace there will be no end, on the throne of David and over his kingdom, to establish it and to uphold it with justice and with righteousness from this time forth and forevermore. The zeal of the LORD of hosts will do

this.

For unto Believers is a Human child born, for unto Believers is a divine Son given and His name shall be called "Wonderful Counselor", "Mighty GOD", "Everlasting Father", and the "Prince of Peace". His royal power will continue to grow; and He (GOD) is no longer at war with sin. Jesus will rule as King, David's successor, basing his power on righteousness and justice, from now until the end of time. The LORD Almighty is determined to do all this. What do we do with this incredible love from our GOD?

It is the combination of grace, faith, and the Holy Spirit that allows the abundant life of Christ to manifest itself in Believers. It is not all faith in Jesus Christ, nor is it all the grace of God that manifests itself in the abundant life given Believers, nor can the abundant life happen without receiving the gift of the Holy Spirit. **The life,** Jesus died to give believers, is manifest in the Believer that is humble, understanding the Believer's place in GOD's world, compassionate to the people in need, and bold in following the Holy Spirit. A Believer combines the actions of life, with the power of the "love of GOD", into everyday situations to bring glory to our redeemer and is our good service to a magnificent GOD.

Stop and think about the abundant life described in John 10:11,
        … Jesus is come that you might have life and have it more abundantly.

Do you consider "your life" to be the very abundant life? What would make your present life, "the more abundant life"?
        The abundant life is available to Believers who will act on the unstoppable power of GOD's word, with the leadership of the Holy Spirit of GOD inside Believers,

through the authority given to Believers by Jesus Christ and Almighty GOD, for the benefit of others.

A Believer indwelt with the Holy Spirit is an authorized dealer of the manifestation of GOD's grace to be dealt to others as blessings.

Grace and Faith
Must be in combination to be effective.

The Spiritual forces of grace and faith are symbolized and are combined in everything God created. The reproduction system GOD created for every tree, plant, animal, human, and fish; has a male and a female gender. The perpetual reproduction of the living things on earth is the combination of grace, faith, and a word from GOD, and the proof is the fruit of GOD's world continuing to produce, from creation to right now.

Faith and Grace is the combination that is;

> Jesus saw a multitude and had compassion (faith) for them and healed their sick (grace).
>
> **Abraham (faith) and Sarah (Grace) and a word from GOD, "You shall have a child this next year with Sarah. And Abraham considered not his own body (faith) past the age of childbearing nor the deadness of Sarah's womb (grace) but believed GOD's word and a miracle child was born.**

Faith without grace or grace without faith is not GOD's will for Believers. Think about this;

> God's grace for the Believer does not need the Believer's faithfulness but **needs the Believer to believe in God's faithfulness.**
>
> Believers are not faithful and will not be faithful, but

GOD is faithful, and it is GOD's faithfulness that matters.

The new covenant was made between GOD and Jesus, because Jesus is faithful. At the Lord's death, Believers became the beneficiaries of the estate of Jesus Christ.

It was GOD's son who paid the sin debt and it is the Believer's belief in the GOD of Creation, the redemption of His son, and the gift of the Holy Spirit, **that requires your belief** and requires GOD's faithfulness. **Do not allow your behavior in the flesh to keep you <u>from</u> believing and living your identity in Christ Jesus.**

Ephesians 4:24 <u>put off your old self</u>, which belongs to your former manner of life and is corrupt through deceitful desires, and <u>to be renewed in the spirit of your minds</u>, and to put on the new self, created after the likeness of God in true righteousness and holiness.

Hebrews 9:14 How much more shall the blood of Christ, who through the eternal Spirit offered himself without spot to God, **purge your conscience** from dead works <u>to serve the living God?</u>

STOP and use your imagination; everything in Ephesians 4:24 and Hebrews 9:14 must become a mindset in your brain for your mind to be able to put on your "new self" created in the likeness of God. Believer's must believe in the "identity" that you have in Christ sealed by the Holy Spirit. **Do not allow your conscience to condemn you**, Believers must <u>capture and dispel condemning thoughts; you have been forgiven of all sin and GOD does not condemn you.</u> Do not be governed by your emotions or senses, but by the word of GOD. Remember; the spiritual world is more powerful than the physical world. Emotions are reflex actions from pain and anguish or pleasure and happiness without consideration of the Spirit and truth of God's word. Believers must choose to believe GOD and the Bible, instead of what you see or feel with your senses. **Jesus has cleared your conscience before GOD forever.** Listen to the Apostle John tell Believers to reassure our hearts because Believers are the "Truth" and are welcome in front of GOD.

> 1st John 3:19-20 By this we shall know that we (Believers) are of the truth and **reassure our heart** before him; for whenever our heart condemns us, **God is greater than our heart**, and he knows everything Beloved, if you (the Believer's) heart does not condemn us, we have confidence before God;

When fighting thoughts of condemnation, know that condemnation is a lie, STOP and draw from your mind and picture bank, pictures of our magnificent GOD and His love for Believers and take negative thoughts captive. Test words against the dictionary of the word of GOD and dispel thoughts that do not measure up to the word. Do not allow emotions to control your actions. Think about the word of GOD, "Be angry and sin not." That is taking an emotion and controlling it.

A Believer can "only" have faith for promises grace has already fulfilled.

All of the benefits of being in right-standing with GOD are brought to fruition by believing in your right-standing with GOD through Jesus Christ and confessing with our mouth salvation, healing, provision, peace, and deliverance. GOD's grace is sufficient for everything happening in your world, through the Believer's faith, the Holy spirit and the mind of Christ. Think about this; **GOD cannot lie, if GOD made a statement whatever GOD said would be!** If you do not believe the Bible, you are not very smart, because GOD cannot lie. Does gravity work all the time, or does it quit working occasionally? Believers are an heir to all the promises and grace of GOD, appropriated by your faith and a heart filled with love. Expose your mind to the word of GOD to continually renew your mind.

Faith cannot appropriate anything; grace has not made available.

For example, A Believer **is not responsible** for World Peace, or another man's wife, or the money in the banks vault and Believers cannot have faith for items that you have no responsibility to affect.

A Believer is responsible for listening to the Holy Spirit and being led by the Holy Spirit in making a plan for every day. A Believer considering others more significant than himself, is in position to do the works GOD has for Believers to do. Believers are the arms and legs Father GOD uses to fill the needs of the Saints on Earth. **The Holy Spirit has a word of knowledge for Believers every minute of every day, if you ask to be a blessing to someone in need of a good word the Holy spirit will answer. Live your life capturing every moment.**

Listen to the Apostle Paul speak to the Believers about righteousness by faith; It is the Believer's responsibility to believe (faith).

Romans 4:13 For the promise to Abraham and his offspring that he would be heir of the world did not come through the law but through **the righteousness of faith**. For **if it is** the adherents of the law who are to be the heirs, **faith is null and the promise (grace) is void**. For the law brings wrath, **but where there is no law there is no transgression**. That is why it depends on **faith**, in order that the **promise may rest on grace** and be **guaranteed** to all his offspring—not only to the adherent of the law but also to **the one who shares the faith of Abraham,** who is the father of us all, Ephesians 2:8 **For by grace you have been saved through faith.** And this is **not** your own doing; **it is the gift of God.**

Grace is GOD's part
Believers must believe the words you speak (faith)
motivated by the compassion in your heart,
in concert with the Holy Spirit, (grace) and
Belief that, the power of your words
that at your Word
will perform their purpose,
to accomplish GOD's plan.
Believers are GOD's arms and legs,
to deliver answers to needs of the body
and acts of kindness GOD has planned.

The church and denominations have occasionally taught; faith without grace or grace without faith and both teachings are not all of the truth.

Beware of extremes,
Errors in faith and grace teachings.

Remember, it is the combination of GOD's will for your action (grace) and the faith you have in GOD's direction to act in confidence with the Holy Spirit that insures a divine outcome from your actions. The **extremes** of faith and grace are both incorrect principles and will negate divine outcomes, if not combined.

The teaching of grace that leads to error is to believe that GOD is in control of mankind on earth. It is correct to think that God is in control, but GOD chose not to control Mankind. GOD's sovereignty, or GOD is in control, are correct principles, **with the exception,** that On Earth, GOD gave mankind all power over the things under the sea, the things on the earth, the things in the air and most important GOD gave mankind a free will to choose who or what to worship. Genesis 1:26

The error in the teaching of faith is the teaching that Believers must pray, fast, be circumcised, walk holy, worship on the Sabbath, be baptized by submersion, and more edicts to be in right standing with GOD. Denominations, without meaning to; set up new laws, and new points of order, and bring "faith only" teachings back under the law.

Grace is a gift and it is GOD's part and GOD **will not** move on a promise the Believer is seeking because of some effort to be righteous or by some act of the Believer. **Grace is a gift** of GOD.

Both extremes are wrong; the responsibility of each Believer is to prepare the soil of his or her brain to receive GOD's word, as an invisible seed and plant the seed into the soil of our brain and tend or keep the garden of your mind for the growth and watering of that seed. The result of sowing God's word and its growth is a harvest of GOD-centered action, which is a Believer's good service to our Creator, Savior, and Holy Friend.

VERY IMPORTANT; "Faith and Grace" through love is the platform for action and **supply from GOD.** Believers must *understand that without the union of faith and grace for a directed purpose*, **a Believer has no guarantee of the supply** necessary to accomplish the purpose of the faith and grace from the Holy Spirit.

Take a minute to dissect this scripture;

2nd Corinthians 9:8 And God is able (constantly dynamiting) to make all grace abound to you, **so that having all sufficiency in all things at all times, you may abound in every good work.**

How about that scripture for Believers!!! The context of this scripture is giving of yourself and your substance for the benefit of others in the Kingdom of GOD. The Holy Spirit is always with you to deliver supply when Believers are doing acts of kindness for others.

Listen as the Apostle Paul teaches GOD will supply seed to the sower and will multiply seed for the sower and increase the harvest of your righteousness;

> 2nd Corinthians 9:9   As it is written, "He has distributed freely, he has given to the poor; his righteousness endures forever. **"He who supplies seed to the sower and bread for food will supply and multiply your seed for sowing and increase the harvest of your righteousness.** You will be enriched in every way to be generous in every way, which through us will produce thanksgiving to God. **For the ministry of this service is not only supplying the needs of the saints but is also overflowing in many thanksgivings to God.**

The foundation for Believers is to be led by the Holy Spirit to actions of love for the people; your family, church, vocation, and those in need.

For example: Tithing is a pre-cross doctrine and when compelled to tithe, it becomes actions under the law, it negates faith by being taught that tithing brings blessing. **Blessing can only come from GOD; it is not deserved because of your required**

action.

Before you clap or shout hallelujah, at the idea of tithing being pre-cross, the New Covenant of listening to the Holy Spirit, **as to giving,** could test your faith with much larger gifts to the church and those in need, as the Holy Spirit instructs you. If you give according to faith in the word of the Holy Spirit, the blessings will be overwhelming. Giving is a measure of your trust in GOD and no church or denomination should make tithing a requirement, but instead should make listening to the Holy Spirit an implied foundation to every action.

Abraham's life is a good study of grace and faith
And exemplifies faith with grace
and faith without grace.

Abraham and Sarah's names when they received the prophecy of GOD were Abram and Sarai. Abraham is heralded as the first man of faith, but until grace and faith were combined, Abraham (faith) and Sarah (grace) did not produce the fruit of GOD's promise, their son, Isaac. GOD did not prepare the barren womb of Sarah to accept the sperm of Abraham until GOD's timing was right. All along the road to Canaan, Abraham made many missteps just as Believers act outside of the plan of GOD for our lives. Listen to God's prophecy to Abram:

> **Genesis 15:5** And he brought him forth abroad, and said, look now toward heaven, and tell the stars, if thou be able to number them: and he said unto him, So shall thy seed be. **And he believed in the LORD; and (GOD) he counted it to him for righteousness.**

As we begin to look at the combination of faith and grace in the life of Abram and Sarai, we must remember the beginning, GOD chose Abram and Abram agreed to follow GOD, without a destination, and leave his family, but then, Abram brought a group, including his nephew Lott, who would be a stone in his shoe for years, and after arriving in Canaan, at the first sign of a drought Abram went to Egypt instead of inquiring to God for direction and supply.

Listen to GOD's call of Abraham when his name was Abram;
> **Genesis 12:1** The LORD said to Abram, "Leave your country and your people. Leave your father's family and go to the country that I will show you. **I will build a great nation from you.** I will bless you and make your name famous. People will use your name to bless other people. **I will bless those who bless you, and I will curse those who curse you. I will use you to bless all the people on earth."**

The story of Abraham and Sarah is a picture of the combination of grace, faith, and a word from GOD. Abraham's lies and missteps caused incredible problems for the world just as Adam and Eve's sin caused the world to suffer and be separated from GOD. Abram was told to follow the lead of GOD and leave his family but instead:
> Abram brought his nephew Lot, his wife Sarai, and a host of others.
> Abram was led to Canaan but at the first sign of drought, instead of asking GOD for a word Abram bolted to Egypt.
> Abram lied about Sarai being his sister, to save his own life.
> Sarai took Hagar and gave her to Abram, when she thought, she was too old, to produce a son. Trying to help GOD.

Fear of their circumstances caused Abram and Sarai to

doubt the word, GOD had given Abram and Sarai. This doubt caused Abram to deviate from GOD's word and it caused consequences for the world. F-E-A-R False-evidence-appearing-real; Believers are often moved from their appointed direction because of the false evidence presented by the enemy.

Abram's errors caused many consequences

Every time Believers do not follow a word from GOD (grace) and allow their faith to turn to fear, the Believer will not have the result, Believers are wanting to receive. Instead, Believers will receive the consequences of a man-made plan. **Here is the Apostle Paul's description of the two children of Abraham and the two resulting covenants.** Abraham produced two sons one with Hagar (the flesh) and one by miracle conception from a barren wife Sarah (grace). The Apostle Paul in;

> Galatians 4:24-31 says that each son represents a covenant given; one given at Mt. Sinai (Ishmael or the law) and the one given at Mt. Zion in Jerusalem (Isaac, the son of grace).

Listen to these scriptures of Sarai and Eve choosing a wrong direction (man-made plan), in place of following GOD's word:

> Genesis 16:3 And **Sarai Abram's wife took** Hagar, her maid the Egyptian, after Abram had dwelt ten years in the land of Canaan and gave her to her husband Abram to be his wife.
> Genesis 3:6 And when (Eve) the woman saw that the tree was good for food, and that it was pleasant to the eyes, and a tree to be desired to make one wise, **she took** of the fruit thereof, and did eat, and gave also unto her husband with her; and he did eat.

Notice; Sarai and Eve *took* what was not theirs to give and gave it to their husbands and **there were consequences.** God gave both families a promise and both families failed to keep their covenant with GOD and **took what was not theirs** and grace and faith were not merged and there were consequences. One of the consequences of going your own way is God will not be there to supply you with the materials for your man-made solution to a problem. **In the case of Eve,** she believed the fruit of the tree was good to eat, would make her wise, and was pleasant to the eye, but those thoughts were lies from the devil, and GOD's word was true and Eves consequence was death or spiritual separation from GOD's Spirit. **In the case of Sarai,** she tried to help GOD with His promise to Abram for having the son of promise, but adultery with Hagar was not GOD's plan and there was no grace or supply from GOD for "the son of promise" with Hagar. There also was a consequence of having a son with Hagar, the consequence was that the two Sons and their tribes would forever be at odds with each other. The Arabic tribes fathered by Ishmael have always been at odds with Israel.

There was **"no grace"** involved in Abraham having a child, by the Bondwoman, "the promise of GOD" **did not come until the Faith of Abraham was mixed with Sarah (Grace) and belief in the word of GOD,** that Isaac was born. Abraham **produced both children;** the child from the bondwoman was produced with a combination of **faith and the flesh,** but the child, Isaac, was from the **miraculous conception** with Sarah (grace) and the faith of Abraham. GOD's promise was supernaturally produced from a barren woman over ninety years of age.

Today, if Believers **do not** combine "faith and grace" with a word from GOD, the abundant life will not manifest. **Grace is not a thing, grace is a person; Jesus Christ is grace and truth and His Spirit has come to abide with you.** Listen to the

Apostle Paul in Corinthians speak about the importance of the relationship of man and woman and intimacy with mankind and GOD, the picture of the proper combination of faith and grace.

> 1st Corinthians 6:15-20 Do you not know that your bodies are members of Christ? Shall I then take the members of Christ and make them members of a prostitute? Never! Or do you not know that he who is joined to a prostitute becomes one body with her? For, as it is written, "The two will become one flesh." **But he who is joined to the Lord becomes one spirit with him.** Flee from sexual immorality. Every other sin a person commits is outside the body, but the sexually immoral person sins against his own body. **Or do you not know that your body is a temple of the Holy Spirit within you, whom you have from God? You are not your own, for you were bought with a price. So glorify God in your body.**

This scripture is so important and needs meditation to receive its full meaning. Look at all the elements of intimacy with GOD and the problems of missteps with intimacy with anything other than GOD, subtle items like football, excessive workouts, work, etc. can sidetrack your destiny. Believers have been purchased for a very high price and adopted into God's family, Jesus is our brother and we are the Temple of the Holy Spirit. Receiving the knowledge of this kind of love will lead to right living from gratitude for what has been done for you. Beware, Right living out of fear, with condemnation, is against scripture. Right living must come from experiencing the love of GOD and Jesus Christ and desiring to live right. Grace is not behavior modification but is transformation by the renewing of your mind to the things of GOD.

Trying to get ahead of GOD
Caused consequences for Abraham and the world.

Genesis 20: This chapter is a picture of **Faith and Grace** and the consequences of removing grace from faith: Abraham was similar to Believers in that his **faith had rendered him righteous;**

* despite his lie to Abimelech that Sarah was his sister,
* despite bringing his Nephew Lot to Canaan,
* and despite having a child with Hagar.

Believers are saved by grace through faith and God does not count Believer's sins against them; GOD counts the direction of your heart. Now let us look at the story of the Abrams trip to Egypt, that was determined by Abram not GOD. When Abimelech, King of Egypt, spotted the beauty of Sarai, he wanted her for his harem, Abraham lied and said she was his sister so that Abimelech did not just kill him and take Sarai, and King Abimelech took Sarai. Abimelech took **grace** (Sarah) from **faith** (Abraham) for the wrong reason (lust) and put her in his harem. GOD did not allow Sarai to be intimate with Abimelech.

The marriage of **grace to faith;** grace is not to be used, but instead grace is part of God and we need to be intimate with Grace. **It is the union and intimacy of "Faith" and "Grace" that produces the successful works of GOD and the abundant life in the Kingdom of GOD on earth, right now.** In the story, of Abraham and Abimelech, GOD did not allow Abimelech to be intimate with Sarah, GOD came to Abimelech in a dream and said

> "Thou are a dead man for the woman thou hast taken is a man's wife. Abimelech replied, but God they lied, and I am innocent, God continued, now restore Abraham his wife (grace) for he (faith) is a Prophet and he shall pray

for you and you shall live" (grace)…..
The next morning Abimelech brought many gifts of
animals and silver and restored Sarah **(grace)** to
Abraham **(faith)** and **Abraham prayed for Abimelech
and he was healed fast of all the sores and his whole
family and servants and their wombs were opened,
and they produced. Genesis 20:3-18**

**Very important first mentions in the Bible,
GOD spoke those things which be not,
as though they were.**

Notice: This is the first mention of Abraham being a Prophet in
verse 7, and first mention of healing in verse 17, and the first
mention of prayer for healing in verse 17. When Grace and Faith
were united "the prayer for the sick" produced healing.

Abraham and Sarah were brother and sister, of the same father,
but not of the same mother, but Abraham was trying to deceive
Abimelech, when he told Abimelech that Sarah was his sister.
And yet, GOD used an imperfect man whose faith was counted
as righteousness to pray for the **sick, to bless the wombs of
Abimelech's family and flocks, when Abraham had no
children and Sarah seemed barren.**

Note: Abraham, who was without children, prayed for
Abimelech and the wombs of the family, slaves, and flocks of
Abimelech were all healed, and **their wombs were opened,** and
they had children, flocks, and herds.

This is an Old Testament recording of **the first prayer for the
sick** and **barren** and their healing and the prayer was
administered by a flawed man who in the sentence before had
lied and allowed his wife to be taken, but Abraham, because of

his belief in God, was considered righteous. **God intervened.** This story from the Old Testament is important to Believers, to show that flawed humans, who are saved and received the Holy Spirit are in right standing with God and can combine being led by the Spirit, with faith in GOD's plan, and give away GOD's grace to minister to people in need of opening their wombs, healing, salvation, or freedom from the enemy. Believers have the Spirit of GOD inside Believers, to unite us with power for good works above all that we can ask or think. (Ephesians 3:20)

When GOD Almighty changed the names of Abram and Sarai to Abraham and Sarah, GOD added the Hebrew letter representing "Grace" to each name. The letter "Hey" is the fifth letter of the Hebrew alphabet and represents grace and is used twice in the Name of God Yud-Hey-Vav-Hey (Jehovah).

**Every problem in life results
from a wrong Spiritual choice.
Every choice ends in a Spiritual solution
or the consequence of a man-made solution.**

Every perceived problem, for Abraham and Sarah and all Believers, results from **not** having consulted GOD, in your planning, prior to the problem. Many perceived problems are the result of a personal goal, not achieved; which is not a problem of a GOD blessed plan. Jesus has agreed to be your shepherd and lead Believers and has assured Believers that He will speak to Believers and they will hear His voice. (John 10) Think about it, Believers leave the grace of GOD when they operate in their own understanding.

> You **do not have** a sin problem; you have a consequence of the flesh.
> You **do not have** a health problem; you have a belief problem.

You **do not have** a provision problem but an <u>unbelief problem</u>.

The reason all problems are Spiritual is that the answer to all problems is answered in the three aspects of our GOD and their finished works.

Think about the origin of problems;

Do you have a problem because your situation is not what you had planned? Did the Holy Spirit bless your plan?

Do you have an idea what GOD wants, you to do, today?

When is the last time you spoke to GOD and what advice <u>did</u> He give you? Or did you act without a word from GOD?

If your plan for today, did not start with worship, praise, and thanksgiving to GOD Almighty, will your plan include a word from the Holy Spirit, a word from the Bible, or compassion in your heart for a person in need; you will not be in the center of GOD's will for your day, and you have no right or promise to expect GOD's supply for an action outside of GOD's purpose.

Let us take a minute, to think about the grace and faith of a marriage. Think about your prayer for your marriage relationship today: Don't pray for your spouse to change to make your marriage better, pray for wisdom to know the path you need to walk to make your marriage better. It is your job in the marriage to pray for and serve your wife and it is her job to pray for and serve the husband. When both partners in a marriage answer to GOD for their actions, "each day" there will be harmony in the home because there is no judgment in the home. Instead of judging your spouse, judge yourself and your marriage will be blessed. The combination of grace and faith will unite the two of you to become one in union with GOD. GOD's wisdom is the way to begin every day and every action. You and your wife were created to be one, listen to this scripture about the creation of man and woman and realize it is faith and grace and a word from GOD that makes a couple one;

> Genesis 5:1 In the day that God created man, in the likeness of God made he him; **male and female created he <u>them</u>; and blessed <u>them</u>, and called their name <u>Adam</u>**, in the day when they were created.

Do not miss the importance of this scripture, the way for a marriage to be "one" is for faith of the couple and the grace of GOD to be intimate. The most common division between man and woman and between mankind and GOD is the pursuit of money as an idol, instead of happiness from a relationship with GOD.

Listen to this story of Solomon, and his fall, when he left his commitment to GOD and allowed idols in his house.

Solomon's request of GOD
exposed his motivation to be in the will of GOD.

> 1st Kings 3:9 **Give your servant therefore an understanding mind to govern your people, that I may discern between good and evil,** for who is able to govern this your great people?" *It pleased the Lord* that Solomon had asked this. And God said to him, "Because you have asked this, and have not asked for yourself **long life or riches** or the life of your enemies but have asked for yourself <u>understanding to discern what is right</u>, behold, I now do according to your word.

Behold, I give you a wise and discerning mind, so that none like you has been before you and none like you shall arise after you. **I give you also what you have not asked, both riches and honor, so that no other king shall compare with you, all your days.** _And if you will walk in my ways_, keeping my statutes and my commandments, as your father David walked, then I will lengthen your days."

Solomon failed to keep the Lord's statutes having a 1,000 wives and Solomon allowed his wives to keep their idols and consequently died early as the richest man that ever lived, but lived, without the relationship, with GOD, that was available. Idolatry or self-righteousness will separate you from GOD. In contrast, David, Solomon's father, was a flawed man with a heart and mind focused on GOD and was praised by GOD, but the idolatry of Solomon caused an early death, just as GOD declared when GOD blessed Solomon.

Idolatry separates mankind from GOD, (the choice; who or what do you trust?) those who get up every morning to go to work to store up money or Believers who get up and want to know what God wants for your day, as the Believer goes to their vocation. The question with money is "not about money" but against living in the currency of the visible world or alternatively living in the currency of the Spiritual world, which is trust in GOD. The scripture says, No Steward can serve two masters. Even when, Believers forget to include the wisdom of the Holy Spirit in our plan and wind up in a ditch, **Believers can regain control of our thoughts** and ask the Holy Spirit for wisdom for getting out of the ditch. The word of the Lord reveals that "trust in God for provision" or "trust in the systems of money", **is the choice**? GOD will help you get out of the ditch, but the ditch always leaves scars or consequences. GOD had a better way, than by way of the ditch.

**Wisdom to know the difference
between GOD and evil
or Good and evil.**

Staying in the plan of GOD, with leadership from the Holy Spirit is the only way to stay GOD-centered in the Kingdom of GOD. The way of the self-centered is filled with opportunities to be confronted with demonic influence. Emotions have no basis in Believers and will cause strife, that is why it is so important to act and be moved by the word of GOD. Listen to the story of the Apostle Peter and his well-intentioned misstep. In the 16th chapter of Matthew, we can see Peter **praised** for his revelation of "who Jesus is" and then **rebuked** a few verses later for thinking that he, Peter, could prevent the plan of GOD from advancing Jesus to the cross. This sets up the underlying problem of Peters actions within a few verses and gives Believers a look at ourselves when we step out of GOD's plan. Peter was trying to be a good soldier, for his leader; just as Believers are trying to follow GOD. Believers can allow, our timing, to get in the way of GOD's planning, just like Peter. Believers using worldly wisdom and action instead of a spiritual solution will not have divine outcomes. *Remember every problem we face needs a Spiritual evaluation and reaction or there will **not** be supply from GOD.*

Listen to Jesus point out the difference between "Trust in the Lord" and "trust in the world system" with the Apostle Peter;

> Matthew 16:15 He (Jesus) said to them, "But who do you say that I am?" Simon Peter replied, "**You are the Christ, the Son of the living God.**" And Jesus answered him, "**Blessed are you, Simon Bar-Jonah! For flesh and blood has not revealed this to you, but**

my Father who is in heaven. And I tell you, you are Peter, and on this rock (of revelation) I will build my church, and the gates of hell shall not prevail against it.

Peter is listening to God and getting revelation of who Jesus is. Peter is given a word of knowledge from the Spirit.

Six verses later;

Jesus Foretells His Death and Resurrection

Matthew 16:21 From that time Jesus began to show his disciples that he must go to Jerusalem and suffer many things from the elders and chief priests and scribes, **and be killed, and on the third day be raised.** And Peter took him aside and began to rebuke him, saying, "Far be it from you, Lord! **This shall never happen to you.**" But he (Jesus) turned and said to Peter, "*Get behind me, Satan!* You are a hindrance to me. **For you are <u>not</u> setting your mind on the things of God, but on the things of man.**"

Peter has allowed demonic influence to cloud his vision; Peter is not keeping his mind on things above, but on things on the earth. When Believers act without a word from the Holy Spirit (a revelation) we are not guaranteed a divine outcome.

Acting without a word from GOD, Does not allow grace, faith and a heart of love to combine.

The grace of GOD **will not** act in concert with the flesh. Listen to these scriptures describing being in the plan of GOD with your actions and being drawn away from GOD's plan into a man-made plan;

> James 1:14 But every man is tempted, **when he is drawn away of his own lust, and enticed.** Then when lust hath conceived, it (lust) bringeth forth sin: and sin, when it is finished, bringeth forth death.
>
> Galatians 5:18 But if you are led by the Spirit, you are not under the law. **Now the works of the flesh are evident:** sexual immorality, impurity, sensuality, idolatry, sorcery, enmity, strife, jealousy, fits of anger, rivalries, dissensions, divisions, envy, drunkenness, orgies, and things like these. **I warn you, as I warned you before, that those who do such things will not inherit the kingdom of God.**

Note: any of these emotions in Galatians 5:18 should be a red flag to Believers that they have lost control of their thought life and need to stop and regain control. **Now read the fruit of the New Creation Spirit;**

> Galatians 5:22-23 But **the fruit of the Spirit** is love, joy, peace, patience, kindness, goodness, faithfulness, gentleness, self-control; against such things there is no law.
>
> **Philippians 2:12** Therefore, my beloved, as you have always obeyed, so now, not only as in my presence but much more in my absence, work out your own salvation with fear and trembling, **for it is God who works in you, both to will and to work for his good pleasure.**

When the constant drum beat of your heart is to please GOD and you are immovable, without a word of action from the Holy Spirit, you are at the right place. The focus on GOD does not keep you from being the most exciting person to be around at work or school.

Luke in Acts, writes to the Church and tells the readers of the power of the Gospel of Grace of Jesus Christ.

Gospel of Grace

> Acts 13:44-46 The next Sabbath almost the whole city gathered to hear the word of the Lord. So they (disciples) remained for a long time, speaking boldly for the Lord, who bore witness to the **word of his grace,** granting signs and wonders to be done by their hands. And now I commend you to God and to the word of his grace, which is able to build you up and to give you the inheritance among all those who are sanctified (set apart in their motivation to GOD).

Again, listen and bury in your heart and mind: these verses concerning life with and without the Holy Spirit;

> 2nd Corinthians 3:17 **Now the Lord is the Spirit, and where the Spirit of the Lord is, there is freedom.** And we all, with unveiled face, beholding the glory of the Lord, **are being transformed into the same image from one degree of glory to another.** For this comes **from the Lord who is the Spirit.**
> 2nd Timothy 1:6 For this reason I remind you to fan into flame the gift of God, which is in you through the laying on of my hands, for **God gave us a spirit** *not of fear* but of **power and love and self-control.**
> 2nd Corinthians 3:2 **Ye are our epistle written in our hearts, known and read of all men:** *Forasmuch as ye are* manifestly declared to be the epistle of Christ ministered by us, written not with ink, but with the Spirit of the living God; not in tables of stone, but in fleshy tables of the heart.
> Revelation 21:7 **The one who conquers will have this**

heritage, and I will be his God and he will be my son. But as for the cowardly, the faithless, the detestable, as for murderers, the sexually immoral, sorcerers, idolaters, and all liars, their portion will be in the lake that burns with fire and sulfur, which is the second death."

GOD's grace is sufficient for every need in your life; the Believers mindset must focus **on the abundance of grace** and *not the appearance of a need*. Thinking about the need stifles the power of the abundance of God's grace. GOD's will is, for the motivation of your faith actions, to depend on GOD's grace for supply. Believers must come to the end of yourself, to find the beginning of GOD. GOD will not share the throne of your life, with you. (Romans 12:1-2) Having the Holy spirit active in your body will make you smart, loving, caring, insightful, powerful, and kind; if you depend on GOD for motivation of your actions.

Notes

THE JOURNEY TO DISCOVER GOD.

CHAPTER 2

Your imagination produces images of what you can't see.

A positive imagination is very important to Believers to visualize the invisible world of GOD. The Kingdom of GOD is inside the Believers and is part of the eternal world and must be imagined for the Spiritual eyes to be enlightened. Words of the Bible and Christianity must be conceived, birthed and nurtured in your brain to be available to be drawn out by your mind and activated for reaction to the issues of life. For example; The Believer must know that the Lord has given Believers his peace and Believers must have a conception of the peace to be able to call on the peace when needed. A seed of GOD's love; thought or imagined in your mind, must be planted in your brain and nurtured for a time to allow your confidence in the word of GOD to grow into brain mindsets as knowledge of GOD. The knowledge of GOD's word will reassure your heart, with confidence. GOD's word creates and will shape the mindsets in your brain so that **the mind** can call on the brain mindsets to react to the issues of life. Remember; your mind controls the brain and every ten seconds sweeps the thoughts and makes decisions to keep thoughts and act or to discard the thoughts.

When Believers ask and receive the gift of the Holy Spirit, to live inside Believers; (Luke 11:13) Almighty GOD, the Creator, and Jesus Christ, the Redeemer, come with the Holy Spirit to the Temple inside Believers because our GOD, is one GOD. Think about it, Almighty God is inside you.

What does your mind "imagine" when you hear the words of the Bible; "*Yetser*" translated for "mind" means conception, or imagination. In the old testament, "yester" and "dianoia" translated for "mind" in the new testament, defined as imagination or deep thought in the verse," love God with all your **mind**". Remember your mind tells the brain how it wants the body to function and what to do with the up to 180,000 thoughts you have each day.

Does the Bible say anything about GOD's imagination; the answer is yes, listen to what GOD said to Jeremiah, about mankind? Jeremiah 1:4-5 and also David in Psalms 139:13;

Jeremiah 1:4 Now the word of the LORD came to me, saying, "Before I formed you in the womb **I knew you, and before you were born I consecrated (set you apart) you;** I appointed you a prophet to the nations." Psalms 139:13 You alone created my inner being. **You knitted me together inside my mother. I will give thanks to you because I have been so amazingly and miraculously made.** Your works are miraculous, and my soul is fully aware of this. My bones were not hidden from you when I was being made in secret, when I was being skillfully woven in an underground workshop. Your eyes saw me when I was only a (embryo) fetus. Every day of my life was **recorded in your book** before one of them had taken place.

Notice and realize; both scriptures exemplify that thoughts can operate outside time and space and are significantly greater than sense knowledge.

The Bible is the greatest picture book and gives all Believers a glimpse of GOD and the Kingdom of GOD inside Believers. Believers must grow our imaginations to include the Spiritual world. Exploring the creation of the world with your imagination builds faith in GOD Almighty and is a start to communicating with the Holy Spirit. Everyday **stop,** to imagine something new and ask the Holy Spirit about its creation.

Listen to the following words of Jesus giving Believers word pictures to imagine and ponder to understand.

> **Jesus said,** I am the bread of life: he that cometh to me shall never hunger; and he that believeth on me shall never thirst. John 6:35
>
> In the last day, that great *day* of the feast (of Tabernacles), **Jesus stood and cried,** saying, If any man thirst, **let him come unto me, and drink.** He that believeth on me, as the scripture hath said, **out of his belly shall flow rivers of living water. John 7:37**
>
> **Jesus said,** I am the light of the world: he that followeth me **shall not** walk in darkness but shall have the light of life. John 8:12
>
> **Jesus said,** I am the door: by me if any man enters in, he shall be saved, and shall go in and out, and find pasture. John 10:9
>
> **Jesus said** unto her, I am the resurrection, and the life: he that believeth in me, though he were dead, yet shall he live: John 11:25
>
> **Jesus saith** unto him, I am the way, the truth, and the life: no man cometh unto the Father, but by me. John 14:6
>
> **Jesus said,** I am the vine, ye *are* the branches: He that abideth in me, and I in him, the same bringeth forth much fruit: for without me ye can do nothing. John 15:5
>
> **Jesus said,** all the churches shall know that I am he which searcheth the mind and hearts: and I will give unto every one of you according to your works. Revelation 2:23

Jesus said, I am Alpha and Omega, the beginning and the end, the first and the last. Revelation 22:13
Jesus said, I am the root and the offspring of David, *and* the bright and morning star. Revelation 22:16
Jesus Christ is the same yesterday and today and forever. Hebrews 13:8

Now, listen to the Apostle Paul tell us about the three baptisms of the Israelites coming out of Egypt and the part Jesus played in the deliverance.

> **1st Corinthians 10:1** all were baptized into **Moses** in the **cloud** and in the **sea,** and all ate the same **spiritual food,** and all drank the same **spiritual drink.** For they drank from the **spiritual Rock** that followed them, and **the Rock was Christ**.

Can you create an image for each physical and spiritual descriptions of the Lord? Close your eyes and look into the Spiritual part of your mind, imagine the Lord Jesus Christ giving you the Holy Spirit to be with you and in you. Any situation you face, will have to conform to the Believer's authority, the power of the Holy Spirit, and the attributes of your standing in Jesus Christ.

During the tempting of Jesus by Satan, Jesus resisted and said, "Man shall not live by bread alone but by every word that proceeds out of the mouth of GOD." When you see Jesus as "The Bread of Life", Believers will have provision for physical bread and the abundant life of being a child of Almighty GOD able to resist the enemy at any time with power from outside time. Do you realize your salvation is a blessing from outside time, your sin was forgiven before you were born, your name was written in the, "Lamb's book of Life" 1990 years ago; Believers must grow our mind to understand the Spiritual, virtual world that GOD created.

Minor Problem:
You cannot believe for something
you do not know.

Believers must be able to "*see the object of the words*" **of the Bible.** Reading the Bible is easier to understand when you develop definitions of the words seldom used in our culture but are active in the Bible. Listen, imagine, and conceive the picture of these words of God, so that you will understand and know what they look like when you hear, see, or read them; in the same way that when you see, hear, or read C-A-R you have a picture of the word. Believers must use your spiritual eyes to set up pictures in your brain. Think about this scripture;

> Ephesians 1:18 **The eyes of your understanding** being enlightened; that ye may know what is the hope of his calling, and what the riches of the glory of his inheritance in the saints,

The Apostle Paul is informing you that you can see with your understanding of GOD as well as with your physical eyes. Now picture, understand, recognize, and set up mindsets in your brain of these words so that the Bible will be more instructive, as you meditate on GOD's word. This is, "who you are in Christ Jesus".

Just Imagine

Justified: Just-as-if-I-had-never sinned; righteous, cleared to be in God's presence, imagine Jesus grabbing your hand and walking into the throne room of GOD and saying this is My brother or My sister.

Repentance; Picture taking off the rags of man's ability and putting on the righteous covering of GOD. Dedicating your mind to doing good and not evil and to follow a GOD-centered motivation for every word or action. Changing your mind and/or direction to see where GOD is going and follow GOD.

Salvation; Asking and "**knowing without a doubt**", believing that you have received total forgiveness through the sacrifice of Jesus Christ. You did nothing to deserve Salvation and there is nothing you can do to lose Salvation. **Imagine your skin is transparent and you can see the Temple, GOD made inside you** for your Born-again Spirit and GOD's Holy Spirit to be together.

Inheritance of the Saints; Imagine, The Lord's blood redeemed the Believer's sin, His stripes healed our diseases, on His shoulders He bore our sorrows and carried our griefs, He was pierced for our transgressions, His body was bruised for our iniquities, He was punished to bring us peace, and He was made poor that we might become rich. Isaiah 53 and 2nd Corinthians 9:8-11

Redeemed; Imagine a large, "*Paid in Full stamp*". The curses of being your own god are gone, no longer are you from Adam and Eve's side of the family but now you have been adopted by GOD Almighty. The cost of your adoption has been "**paid in full**" by Jesus. You have been brought home by Jesus to the Fathers house and Father GOD has adopted you and given you His name. Jesus is your big brother.

Grace and Faith; Grace is like the sun and faith is like a skylight in your house. The sun or GOD's grace is the most significant force in the universe and your faith allows the light and warmth of the grace of GOD into your life through the skylight of the Believer's faith. This picture shows that the grace of GOD is everywhere, and you do not have to work for it. Instead of work, you have to believe and let grace shine in your life through seeing Jesus in His loving service to Believers.

Sin is living unto yourself and filling, the GOD made void, in your life with a man-made god of your choosing that fits with your lifestyle. Lawlessness is living without a moral code. Beware, you can make a man-made god for your life that fits your lifestyle, even at church.

Sanctified; Believers have been made Holy by Jesus Christ and set apart for GOD. "**Saint-ified**" Imagine a fuel tank gauge showing empty and being filled with Jesus and the knowledge of GOD until it reads full of Jesus. The active lifestyle of a Believer is to bring glory to GOD every day. The Believer's spirit was made holy by the elimination of the universe of sin, through the payment for all sin and taking punishment for all the wrath of the Father, absorbed by Jesus Christ.

Prayer; picture your I phone and rename your phone the "I am" phone. With the same fervor that you depend on your phone, that is the fervor that represents prayer, when Paul said pray "unceasingly". Prayer is communication with GOD in all forms; worship, praise, requests, listening, conversing, and prayer is the attitude for living with GOD in leadership of your life.

Imagine; You need to know; where you are going, who are you going to meet, if you're having lunch, who is going to drive, what should you wear, who is going to pay, are we meeting anyone, and **Who better to ask to bless your plan, than the Holy Spirit?**

When these words are nurtured and grow into brain-mindsets as knowledge of GOD, your mind can draw on them when needed to capture thoughts, corral emotions and act with power. The Lord has given Believers a spirit of love, a spirit of power, and a sound mind.

The brain is filled with knowledge from thoughts and when the right thoughts are firmed up by meditation and repetition, the thoughts produce brain-mindsets and when **the mind** instructs the brain to activate **a mindset, the substance in the words will perform the function GOD designed in the words.** Listen as the Apostle Paul describes the power of our mind to determine the quality of our life;

> 2nd Corinthians 10:4 For the weapons of our warfare are not of the flesh but **(Believers) have divine power to destroy strongholds.** We destroy (chaos) arguments and every lofty opinion raised against the knowledge of God, **and take every thought captive to obey Christ**, being ready to punish every disobedience, when your obedience is complete.

When you control your emotions (thought life) you control your life. Everything about this scripture is in the Spiritual world, outside time, with your mind calling for the authority given Believers at Creation and the Cross. Do not miss the declaration that Believers **are not** fighting with **flesh and blood** but *against arguments raised against Jesus Christ.*

**Words were created by GOD
to execute their function.**

Wisdom is the proper use of the knowledge of GOD. Words are the force driving wisdom and evil. Words are filled with power from the platform from which they were spoken. Words spoken, from the standing given Believers by Jesus Christ, through the Holy Spirit will perform their function according to the power in the word, given the word, by GOD.

GOD used invisible building blocks to make matter and create life. Mankind is affected by DNA, gravity, atoms, molecules, and things that are not visible. **Jesus inhabits and controls the unseen world to maintain the harmony of the world designed and created by GOD including words.** Jesus is controlling the unseen world. The atoms, inside all matter are moving at incredible speed and Jesus is the force to control their power. GOD really does have, **"The whole world in His Hands"**.

> **Hebrews11:6** But without *belief in GOD* it is* impossible to please GOD: for he that cometh to God must believe **that GOD is,** and *that* GOD is a rewarder of them that diligently seek him.
> The word, Believe, is the combination of "Be" and "Live". You will live, what you are on the inside, in your "being".

Believers can expand and develop our imagination to unlock a more complete picture of GOD and establish, who Believers are by meditating on the word of GOD. Your brain will produce energy from mindsets, which the mind can use to create and establish your faith. The Holy Spirit and the Believer's mind can do things beyond what we ask or think with the power of words and the grace of GOD who created meaning in the words we speak. Remember; GOD said, "Let there be light", and Jesus said, "Wind be still" and Paul said, "Rise up and walk" and the action happened after they spoke, **things that were not became things that are.**" And GOD is the same yesterday, today, and forever. (Hebrews 13:8)

>The miracles of GOD show that Jesus was **more powerful than time, for example;** at the wedding in Cana, in the first miracle of turning water into fine wine, Jesus accelerated the aging process for wine in an instant.

>The next miracle in the town of Cana confirmed the Lord's **power over space** as He healed the Centurion's son twenty miles away in Capernaum. GOD's word is more powerful than time and space and Jesus used words to create both miracles. Believers baptized with the Holy Spirit are not bound by time and space in the realm of the Spirit. Remember, your salvation was waiting on you for 1990 years. Salvation is outside time in the eternal realm.

Every Believer looks at GOD's Creation, eats from GOD's creation, breathes air from GOD's creation, and uses GOD's creation for the foundation of their vocation. What do you see or imagine when Elohim, GOD, spoke the world into existence? Genesis 1-2 and Job 38 are two of the descriptions of the creation. Consider this: Everyone is dedicated to and worships the god in their life. Christians worship the one and only Savior GOD to the world.

Do not allow the theory of evolution to enter you mind, it is not the truth, you can verify this fact by looking at the function of your eyes and trying to imagine, how a one cell creature grew to be you.

>Your eyes are driven by 130 million light sensitive receptor impulses to a photo chemical reaction that

transforms light into electrical impulses that go to the brain to produce pictures of what you are seeing, many times faster than the speed of light.

The Christian life is enhanced if you believe in creation, of the worlds, by GOD, along with salvation through belief in Jesus Christ. The Believer who does not believe in creation will suffer roadblocks on the avenue of GOD's love. Creation was an act of love from an Almighty GOD, for a people, who can choose to love the "Creator of All" and be loved by GOD Almighty. Redemption for the world was made available by Jesus Christ and was an act of love from Father GOD who said,

> "For God so **loved the world** that He gave His only Son that whosoever believeth in Him, **shall not perish,** but have eternal life."

Imagination is the beginning of seeing the invisible world including the Kingdom of GOD. The human brain is a storage bank for images that have been imagined, seen, and images not yet imagined.

> Some images come as a result of the environment, physical needs, and what you see, hear, touch, and feel. Some imaginations are traumatic and create chaos for the brain and must be overridden by love in your heart and the word of GOD.
>
> The basis for positive mindsets: love, kindness, joy, peace, gentleness, the presence of GOD with us, and more are part of the invisible Kingdom of GOD inside Believers who believe.

The Bible was written in images that must be imagined and seen with the mind and put into your heart because they are invisible, but they are powerful and have substance to those who believe GOD. Consider this; The images you see, with your eyes, were made by GOD speaking things into existence. The Believer's mind can draw upon the knowledge of GOD in your heart and activate words of faith for acts of kindness planned by GOD.

**Wrong living comes through wrong believing.
The enemy is trying to lead you through your conscience.**

GOD and fear are both forces that are invisible and must be imagined.

- Faith is belief in GOD and His creation and based on love.
- Fear is the opposite of faith in GOD; fear is the imagining of failure, physical harm, pain, death, disease, etc. from your senses. **Picture this acronym F-E-A-R**
- **False-Evidence-Appearing-Real.**

Your identity as a child of GOD is 1990 years old; **you were saved, healed, delivered, and given standing to enforce GOD's laws of the New Covenant at the cross.** Believers have an identity in Jesus Christ sealed by the Holy Spirit inside the Believer. Believers, living on the positive side of your imagination, can stop thoughts that yield fear by concentrating on the word of GOD and the images of truth you have stored in your heart. What is **your image** of "shall not perish" from John 3:16, the scripture above?

The definition of "**Shall not perish**" is shall not be marred or lose, "shall not perish" is present tense for right now, not when you reach Heaven. "Shall not perish" starts at the same time as your "Born-again Spirit came to eternal life, when you believed.

Believers must constantly renew our minds to keep mindsets of peace and dispel thoughts of chaos. Remember you will not need the phrase, "shall not perish" in Heaven and the phrase is not in the future tense. It is for right now. Every human has an internal need to know "The Creator" of the world and everyone is tempted or bullied by the enemy. If the Believer's imagination of GOD is greater than the power to bully, by Satan, the Believer **will not** be bullied or condemned. The Believer's relationship with GOD comes from the imaging of GOD's word and personal communication with the Holy Spirit inside Believers. It is our destiny, to know who made us, and to have a relationship with Jesus Christ, who redeemed us. If you cannot imagine the Spiritual World, you cannot live in the power of GOD, and **use the Believer's authority to enforce GOD's laws of the New Covenant. The Kingdom of GOD is inside Believers** and is ruled by the instructions written in your heart by GOD through the Holy Spirit. It is "Who you are in Christ Jesus".

> **The war GOD had with sin** has been won, the war is over, and Believers have been reconciled to GOD and GOD is not recording sin to mankind. GOD is not upset, mad, or angry at Believers because the payment for sin has been paid and the punishment exacted. Almighty GOD has His Son back at His side and has sent a part of Himself to be in every human who will believe.

Think about this: The Human world is subject to time and deterioration, the Spiritual world controls the Human world, the spiritual world is not subject to time, but is powerful and can affect the physical world. The mind can use the brain to deal with current situations with power from outside time, the mind can work at speeds outside time and operate in the promises of GOD from 1990 years ago at the Cross. Listen to the Apostle Paul;

> 2nd Corinthians 4:18 as we look not to the things that are seen but **to the things that are unseen.** For the things that are seen are transient, but **the things that**

are unseen are eternal.

Notice; The authority and promises from GOD and Jesus Christ to Believers are eternal but restricted to you according to the level of your belief. Think about this; when Believers die the organ called the brain dies with the body but the mind is eternal along with your Born-again Spirit, your mind operates in the invisible world and if the Believer's Spirit is joined with the Holy Spirit there is wonderful power. The invisible spiritual world was before and will be after. The Spiritual, invisible, world controls all the molecules, atoms, reproduction systems of all the plants and trees, fish and animals, and mountains and oceans, et cetera. Remember; the Kingdom of GOD inside Believers, with all the power and invisible underpinnings of the world, that GOD put into motion at creation and Jesus finished at the cross. Think about the miracles of mind over matter when Jesus passed through the locked door of the upper room without opening it, or Phillip disappearing after he baptized the Eunuch.

Listen to the Apostle Paul tell Believers how to reach into the Spiritual world with actions prompted from a heart of compassion, spoken with words of faith, and a push from the Holy Spirit;

> Romans 10:9 That if thou shalt **confess with thy mouth** the Lord Jesus and shall believe in thine heart that God hath raised him from the dead, thou shalt be saved. For with the heart man believeth unto righteousness; and **with the mouth confession is made unto salvation.**

This verbal proclamation, is not an exercise but, is a miracle of resurrection power and operates to appropriate the grace of GOD stored up for Believers, from the death and resurrection of Jesus Christ. This miracle of reconciliation is outside time; Your mind has realized you need a GOD in your life and your mind has looked at the death and resurrection of Jesus as payment for your reconciliation to GOD and the Believer has put Jesus on the throne of your life.

**Receiving through believing
and speaking what you believe.**

All of the promises of Jesus Christ are appropriated in the same way we receive salvation. Without being legalistic but confirming the importance of experiencing the totality of salvation by believing in your heart and **voicing the words** of action from your spirit.

     For example;

              A seeker of GOD, with help from the Holy Spirit, must imagine **their personal need for a Savior.**

              Then the Believer must imagine the love of GOD and horrific sacrifice of Jesus to destroy the power of sin, absorb the punishment for sin, **and bring right-standing with GOD to those who believe.**

              A Christian must believe the sacrifice of Jesus and imagine the benefits of **the inheritance of the saints** from the death and resurrection of Jesus Christ, our Brother.

              And speak that (repentance) change in the direction of your life by announcing your change from self-centered to GOD-centered motivation for your life.

In the brain of a new Believer, GOD Almighty condemned the sin nature and exchanged the sin nature for His righteousness and love. (Romans 8:1-11) The mind of a Believer can now call on the brain to develop mindsets based at their core on the love of GOD given, from before the foundation of the world. Imagine a picture of the lower part of your brain being rich soil and all the good thoughts could lay down in the soil and feel the warmth of the nurturing nutrients of GOD's love. Now imagine the thoughts of the self-centered person and the fearful thoughts of being on your own, the thoughts are like extension cords with nothing on the end but exposed wire popping and jumping around, that is what the brain of an unbeliever looks like. Listen as the Apostle Peter tell us about the knowledge of GOD and its importance in our brain for the mind to call on for life issues;

> 2nd Peter 1:2-4 May grace and peace be multiplied to you in **the knowledge of God and of Jesus our Lord.** His divine power has granted to us all things that pertain to life and godliness, through **the knowledge of him** who called us to his own glory and excellence, by which he has granted to us his precious and very great promises, so that through them (**the promises you know**) you may become partakers of the divine nature, having escaped from the corruption that is in the world because of sinful desire.

The mind of the new Believer must begin to detoxify the Believer's brain of strongholds of strife, selfishness, and chaos with the knowledge of GOD and Jesus Christ. The brain before salvation has a base for decision making steeped in selfishness and is completely self-centered. Turning your motivation for life, over to GOD Almighty; gives the mind a new basis for decision-making based on love, power, and authority. The new view is anchored by the understanding that the world is owned by GOD and the Believer is a steward of GOD's abundance not dependent on your ability but on God's promise and blessing. Listen to the Author of Hebrews telling Believers about the New Covenant after the gentiles have been grafted into the tree of

GOD's people;

> Hebrews 8:10 For this is the covenant that I will make with the house of Israel after those days, declares the Lord: I will put my laws into their minds, and write them on their hearts, and I will be their God, and they shall be my people.

Now; Listen to Jesus describing a Believer's thought life and acting on the Believer's thoughts with our speech and action from Matthew 12

> Matthew 12:35 **A good man out of the good treasure of the heart bringeth forth good things:** and an evil man out of the evil treasure bringeth forth evil things. But I say unto you, that every idle word that men shall speak, they shall give account thereof in the day of judgment. **For by thy words thou shalt be justified, and by thy words thou shalt be condemned.**

The Believer's life must be a constant application of love through spoken words of faith and hope; understanding that spoken words have power and Believers will be judged by their words. The power of the Spiritual world is activated from a compassionate heart, and a brain filled with knowledge of GOD and faith that every word you speak will have power to do what it was designed to do. Words are thought-actions sent from the heart and activated from the mind and should be expected to carry out their substance. For example; A Believer can exchange worry for peace by having your mind call for peace from your brain. The Believer owns the Lord's peace, Jesus gave it to you.

Do not be afraid of the Spiritual world or the Holy Spirit because they are invisible. **Imagine this;** Believers with invisible thoughts fill your hearts with invisible good treasure or evil treasure, and with your motivation of good or evil, bring things out of your heart with invisible words of good or evil. Every person, Believer or unbeliever knows that you can lift someone up with your words or you can blast them to depression with your words. The real power of the world, visible or invisible, is the love of GOD and this love is visible to those acting in love considering others more significantly than themselves. **Important point about GOD's love;** If a Believer gives his love to someone and they do not receive it, the Believer is hurt. When GOD gives His love and it is not received, mankind, who did not receive GOD's love, is hurt. GOD's love is selfless, that is why it is so powerful.

Creating Godly pictures
with your imagination

The Believer's control of your thought life is vital, each thought must be examined to guard your brain from keeping thoughts of evil, just as you guard your stomach and inspect each bite of food to make sure that it is not spoiled. **Every word you speak comes from an image in your mind which flows from the motivation of your heart. GOD gave power to words to complete their function. Picture; joy, peace, tranquility, goodness, sacrifice, and love.** The Devil has a list of words for you also: fear, lust, anger, greed, discouragement, and revenge, the actions of these words need to be harnessed. Remember, Jesus said, "A good man out of the good treasure of the heart brings forth good things" and you know what an evil man brings out of his heart. This can even happen at church. Actions springing from emotions are not a Spiritual road to a divine outcome, Emotions are reactions from happenings in your life of pain or pleasure and neither one is a solid foundation for action. A Believer needs to react from love in the Believer's heart and the truth of the Mind of Christ, not out of reaction to a stimulus of pain or pleasure.

Believers' happiness depends on living in the truth of GOD's word. GOD's word says, that Jesus came to give Believers the abundant life, not the life of condemnation that produces depression, poverty, sickness and death. The root of depression comes from idle words of evil from the heart of the condemned. **Condemnation and sin consciousness are products of unbelief, in the perfect sacrifice of Jesus Christ, and condemning thoughts must be stopped, captured, and thrown out of your brain by your mind.**

Believers must also look for the signs of personal pride; do not think, that Believers have something to do to earn or deserve salvation, healing, or deliverance from depression; those benefits are part of your inheritance as Believers. Jesus paid it all, **there is nothing left for you to** pay. Remember GOD is no longer at war with sin, Jesus has reconciled the Believers to the peace of GOD. If a Believer is experiencing fear in their thought life, they must **stop!** Bring their thoughts under control of their mind and work on detoxing the chaotic thoughts and strongholds in the brain, that are **not in alignment** with the words of Jesus Christ.

Take a minute to imagine this; When you turn on your light switch, you do **not** have to tell the darkness to leave. The love of GOD is the light given to life and darkness is a perpetrator of evil. When you introduce the love of Jesus to your heart you don't have to tell the darkness of evil to leave, it is gone because the light of the GOD is inside you. The light of Jesus, in your heart forever; keeps the darkness from your heart but does not keep your body from breaking the moral code for which there are consequences.

> For example; If you overeat you will be fat whether you are saved or not. If you receive the condemnation of others instead of your powerful position with Jesus Christ, you will be depressed. If you sleep with another

spouse, you can lose your respect in your family and have consequential children.

The Believer's born-again spirit is perfect, but the Believer's body and brain are not perfect. The Believer must use the new creation foundation of GOD's love, in your brain, and the Believer's mind must capture chaotic thoughts and throw them out. A Believer must know, **who you are in Jesus Christ,** to rest in the peace of GOD and **consider not your body** but consider the promise of GOD. The peace of GOD is inside Believers in the person of the Holy Spirit, but you must communicate with the Holy Spirit to activate the peace of GOD. Remember Jesus said, **'Let not your heart** be troubled", **it is your job to guard your heart and not let it be troubled nor let it be afraid....**

> John 16:33 I have said these things to you, that in me you may have peace. In the world you will have tribulation. **But take heart; I (Jesus) have overcome the world."**

Confess with your mouth and believe in your heart and start saying, "Jesus has made me righteous" and "Jesus has overcome the world" and "as Jesus is in this world, so am I".

What is "the more Abundant Life"?

The abundant life stems from Salvation or Total wellbeing. (the Greek word is *sozo*; meaning total wellbeing) In the New Testament "*sozo*" is used 110 times translated as "**saved**" 53 times and 57 times as **total-wellbeing, delivered, or healed. Jesus paid it all; Believers have everything necessary for the abundant life.** Listen to Jesus tell Believers that the life with the Holy Spirit is easy;

> Matthew 11:28 Come to me, all who labor and are heavy laden, **and I will give you rest.** Take my yoke

upon you, and learn from me, for I am gentle and lowly in heart, and you will find rest for your souls. For my yoke is easy, and my burden is light."
Hebrews 4:1 Therefore, while the promise of entering his **rest** still stands, **let us fear** lest any of you should seem to have failed to reach it.(the Lord's rest)

Notice; if you are not "resting" in the peace of GOD you are laboring in your own ability to resolve your burdens. Don't be confused by the word "resting"; think of **resting** as standing in the authority given Believers by Jesus Christ.

The new Covenant is one of power and authority given Believers directed by the Holy Spirit inside Believers for the acts of kindness GOD has for Believers to do.

The Apostle Paul said it best, "It is not I that lives but Christ lives in me and the life I now live in the flesh, I live by faith in the Son of GOD". Galatians 2:20

Almighty GOD is living inside Believers with all the inheritance Jesus died to give Believers but if you do not know about Jesus or your inheritance, it will remain dormant.

Believers cannot believe
something you do not know.

Do you want to know what GOD wrote in your heart and mind as written in Hebrews 8? I believe that the platform of the new creation brain is "Love GOD with all your mind, heart, soul, and strength and your neighbor as yourself". The Believer has received GOD's love, now develop a relationship with the GOD of the Universe, who loves you beyond what you can imagine or think. The Lord's love was given to Believers at the Cross.

Picture what the Lord is saying in John 3;

> John 3:14-15 And as Moses lifted up the serpent in the wilderness, so must the Son of Man be lifted up, that whoever believes in him may have eternal life. (and all who looked on the image were healed)
> John 3:16 For GOD so loved the world that he gave his only begotten son that whosoever believeth in Him **shall not perish** but have everlasting life.
> John 3:17 For God did not send his Son into the world to condemn the world, but in order that the world might be saved (sozo) through him.
> John 3:18 Whoever believes in him is not condemned, **but whoever does not believe is condemned already,** because he has not believed in the name of the only Son of God.
> John 3:36 Whoever believes in the Son has eternal life; **whoever does not obey the Son shall not see life, but the wrath of God remains on him.**

The Gospel announcement of John 3 is of such significance and awe, that the very hearing of the Gospel of Jesus Christ will change a Believer forever. **The revelation of Jesus,** at the Believer's salvation, must be maintained in our daily life by focusing on our relationship by storing up knowledge of GOD in our imagination and brain mindsets. Meditate on the scriptures above to give words, the importance and substance GOD gave the words to accomplish their purpose.

The Holy Spirit is living inside Believers, who ask. GOD is with us and will never leave us, nor forsake us. Does it make any sense or logic for a Believer to act without following the lead of the Holy Spirit and doing everything in word and deed, all in the name of the Lord Jesus? The Lord plans for you to be the best Father, Husband, Mother, Wife, child, Business man or woman,

Homemaker, Friend, Son, Daughter, Neighbor, Athlete, Student, and Steward that you can be, and GOD is with you for comfort and power.

> Do you believe the Holy Spirit will lead you into the ditch or if you end up in the ditch, is the truth you did not ask the Holy Spirit for directions?
>
> Even in the ditch, a Believer can **stop,** regain GODly focus and ask the Holy Spirit for new directions to get out of the ditch.

Listen to this word in Colossians;

> Colossians 3:17 And whatsoever ye do in word or deed, do all in the name of the Lord Jesus, giving thanks to God and the Father by him.

When Believers find themselves in situations that need GOD's help, generally it is due to acting on their own plan without motivation of love in their heart and considering others more significantly than themselves.

Einstein believed in GOD and creation.

Einstein, one of the smartest men, the world has ever known said, "In the view of such harmony in the cosmos which I, with my limited human mind, am able to recognize, there are yet people who say there is no GOD."

> Or in modern terms, "You would have to be an idiot to look at this creation and not believe there was a Creator."

To reign in life as a child of GOD, you must believe in Creator GOD and, the Believer, must understand the victory of Jesus at the Cross and the promise "shall not perish". Believers cannot think they are working for a victory but must remain living in the victory of Jesus, from the cross, 1990 years ago. Think about it, if you are working for a victory you are working in the flesh and if you are working **from** the victory of Jesus Christ, at the cross; you are working outside of time in the Spiritual world with the Holy Spirit and the authority given Believers.

When Moses made the brass serpent for the healing of the Israelites bitten by the poison snakes and lifted it up, everyone that looked upon it was healed of the poison.

When Believers constantly imagine lifting up Jesus, our Savior, and discern or imagine his body sacrificed for Believers, Believers will realize that Believers already own, the blessings of the Lord, including total wellbeing. Salvation will get you to heaven but **the baptism in the Holy Spirit will give Believers the power to reign in life.** Jesus was baptized with the Holy Spirit and He is our example, If Jesus needed the Holy Spirit, how can Believers live without the Holy Spirit? Jesus did not do one miracle until He was baptized in the Holy Spirit. **Do not let stereotypes of the Pentecostal denomination keep you from knowing the Holy Spirit; the Baptism with the Holy Spirit is not weird and will not make you do anything weird.** GOD has given mankind a free will, you are in control, everything in life is the Believer's choice, the Holy Spirit will only interact with you, if you interact with Him. Listen to Jesus;

Luke 11:13 If ye then, being evil, know how to give good gifts unto your children: **how much more shall *your* heavenly Father give the Holy Spirit to them that ask him?**

Let us stop a minute to underscore a point; When a person becomes born-again, they are appropriating the gift of salvation from 1990 years ago. The Lord's sacrifice is 1990 years old, Believers in the post-cross era with the Holy Spirit must live **"from the victory" of Jesus** over the devil, death, hell, and the grave.

Healing, deliverance from depression, and provision must be appropriated in the same way as Salvation. Believers must remember our names **were** written in the, "Lamb's book of Life" not the Lamb's book of death, sickness, depression, hell, and the grave. **The key to understanding the power of salvation is for the eyes of your understanding (imagination) to be active. Believers must see, Almighty GOD's war on sin has been won and settled** with the victory of Jesus over death, hell, and the grave. Believers have been reconciled to GOD by the sacrifice of Jesus. GOD is not angry; God is not even mad. Believers have been given; the Holy Spirit of GOD to reside in them as confirmation of the Lord's victory and to be the executor of the Lord's estate for Believers. Believers were saved, were healed, were delivered, and were made prosperous at the Cross and the words from our mouth must be; I am saved, I am healed, I am the righteousness of GOD in Jesus Christ, and I am delivered. Do not take the word of any created thing or person as to a different identity but the one you have in Jesus Christ.

When Jesus gave Believers His name; Jesus gave Believers his standing in the world, to speak for yourself and for the edification of others with authority to use His name to enforce the instructions GOD has written on your heart.

Conclusion:
Jesus said that Believers hear his voice and Jesus said, that the Holy Spirit would show Believers things to come. If you do not listen to the Holy Spirit you cannot hear and know the things to come. Believers will miss having a "Word of knowledge" for every moment. Believers will have divine outcomes when you act, after you hear from the Holy Spirit about the things to come. When you know what you are **"to be" today** you will be doing

what GOD wants you to do. Listen to the verses from Jeremiah; Jeremiah 29:11 **For I know the plans I have for you,** declares the LORD, <u>plans for welfare and not for evil, to give you a future and a hope</u>. Then you will call upon me and come and pray to me, and I will hear you. You will seek me and find me, when you seek me with all your heart. I will be found by you, declares the LORD, and I will restore your fortunes and gather you from all the nations and all the places where I have driven you, declares the LORD, and I will bring you back to the place from which I sent you into exile.

This is a verse about the Jews returning to Israel, but GOD does not change, He has a plan for every Believer, the question is, are you looking for His plan for your life; this minute, this day, and forever?

CHAPTER 3

Do you know the language of the Holy Spirit?

> Proverbs 4:20 My son, **be attentive to my words;**
> incline your ear to my sayings. **Let them not escape**
> **from your sight;** keep them within your heart. For they
> **are life** to those who **find them,** and **healing to all**
> **their flesh.**

Everything about the "Abundant life", starts with GOD-centered
thoughts and talking to the Holy Spirit and listening for the reply.
The Holy Spirit is the ultimate expression of GOD's love for
you. The promise of the Holy Spirit is to impart grace to
Believers (Hebrews 10:29) and reveal hidden things to come.
(1st Corinthians 2:9-12). Be prepared for the longest sentence in
the book. As you begin to constantly speak to the Holy Spirit all
day every day; praising GOD for the grandeur of the new day,
the majesty of the mountains and oceans, the beauty of the
flowers and trees, the wonder of your body and your eyes, the
power of an Almighty GOD, the love of a Savior, and the
wonderment of the gift of the Holy Spirit to be inside your body
with your Born-again Spirit.

It may be frustrating to you, that you are not often hearing
verbally from the Holy Spirit, but that is because you are trained
to expect an audible word to communicate, do not allow yourself
to be squeezed into the world's mold. You can speak audibly, but
the Holy Spirit is a spirit and will most often Speak to your mind.
The Holy Spirit communicates with your eternal faculties, your

Spirit and your mind are eternal, your body and brain are temporary.

Your relationship with GOD is composed of attending to the love of GOD in your heart and asking, "How can I be the steward, Jesus wants me to be?" You may have seen the colored bracelets with the letters WWJD, "What would Jesus do?" the bracelet idea is a good one. The bracelet is a reminder to constantly think about living the way Jesus would want you to live, but it fell short of the reality of your baptism with the Holy Spirit. **The comforter, the Holy Spirit, sent from GOD to be inside you; for confidence in your identity, power for living in the now, and to reveal things to come is much greater benefit than the bracelet reminder.** The bracelet would not tell you things to come nor bring comfort or power to Believers.

Start your journey to discover GOD.

How can Believers develop a system for depending on the Holy Spirit and GOD's word to reign in life? Believers must start by believing Jesus, when He said," My sheep hear my voice". How do Believers start the relationship with the Holy Spirit? First, you must believe GOD's word that you have been baptized with the Holy Spirit and you must believe that the Temple for your born-again Spirit and the Holy Spirit is inside you. Now, three ways to start your journey;

> Consider others more significantly than your-self before acting.
> Constant two-way communications with the Holy Spirit,
> Develop 3-Dimensional images of GOD and His word.

Step one; For a Believer to be like GOD and to seek first the Kingdom of GOD and His Right-standing, the Believer must consider others more significantly than ourselves, for this is love and GOD is love. GOD's grace and the power of the Holy Spirit is activated from a motivation of love for others.

Step two; Listen as Jesus is telling Believers, that the Holy Spirit will speak to Believers, the words are the Lords, and tell Believers of things to come. Jesus is at the last supper, when He says:

> John 16:12 "I (Jesus) still have many things to say to you, but you cannot bear them **now. When the Spirit of truth (Holy Spirit) comes, he will guide you into all the truth,** for he will not speak on his own authority, but **whatever he hears he will speak, and he will declare to you the things that are to come.** He will glorify me, for he will take what is mine and declare it to you. All that the Father has is mine; **therefore I said that he will take what is mine and declare it to you.**

The Holy Spirit has come and is ready to **declare to Believers** things to come and guide you into all truth. The Holy Spirit is the seal of your identity as a child of GOD, Christian, and part of the family of GOD. The words of Jesus cannot be **understated,** the Holy Spirit has been sent to Believers to declare, speak, and communicate the inheritance of the Lord, given to believers. The Bible declares the following parts of your inheritance;

> I am your redemption.
> I am your blessing.
> I am your health.
> I am your peace.
> I am your brother.
> I am your strength.
> I am your provider.

The "I ams", are word pictures of the Believer's inheritance for right now. Believers can plant the "I ams" in their hearts and minds because the "Great I Am" is abiding with Believers.

> 1st Corinthians 1:30 And because of him you are in Christ Jesus, who became to us **wisdom from God, righteousness and sanctification and redemption,** so that, as it is written, "Let the one who boasts, <u>boast in the Lord.</u>"

GOD is for you, and Jesus has taken away the power of those against you, and Believers have a relationship with the Holy Spirit. Believers are prepared to reign in life according to "How big is your GOD?". If your **GOD is not** more powerful than depression, or headaches, or anxiety or unhappiness, then your life will rise or fall to the level of your belief in GOD. Believers can only access or believe for the promises or the gifts of GOD, **you know about** and believe. Everyone quotes, "The truth will set you free", but the Scripture says, That "If you abide in my word, you are truly my disciples, and you **will** know the truth, and the truth will set you free." John 8:31-32 If you are a disciple and study the word then you will know the truth and then truth will set you free.

Build your Heart for GOD
With images of His mighty works.

Step three; Imagine the GOD of the Bible with virtual pictures stored in your heart, picture your born-again Spirit in your inner being with the Holy Spirit. Jesus has made your New Creation Spirit "perfect" (John 17:23 and Colossians 1:28). It is the meeting and introduction to the Holy Spirit of GOD that is so new and mind-blowing. Believers must jump in the deep end and imagine the experience and speak to the Holy Spirit and by faith break the ice, you have the promise of Jesus that He will speak to you. Start by using your imagination to see the Temple of the

Holy Spirit and your new creation Spirit inside you, in your inner sanctum.

Can you visualize the Biblical accounts of the miracles of GOD? For example, explore, meditate, and create an image of; **The feeding** of the 5,000 with five loaves and two fish and all 5,000 men and families were filled, to their full, with twelve baskets of food left over.
The raising from the dead of Lazarus after being dead four days.
The Apostle Peter's first sermon, after receiving the Holy Spirit, three thousand people were saved, baptized in water, and baptized with the Holy Spirit.
The exodus of the 2 million Israelites from Egypt with millions of dollars in gold and silver and **not a feeble person** in the group and through the opening of the Red Sea to the safety of the other side,

Create other images of the miracles of Jesus and Christ followers, and think about the miracle of the rebirth of the Israel nation in the land GOD gave them, in one day, as an answer to the 2,000+ years old prophecy in Isaiah. The Bible Events are glimpses of the love of GOD for those who believe. These amazing pictures are given to build faith for Believers. Listen to the Apostle Paul talk about our inner ability to see into the Spiritual world;

Ephesians 1:17 that the God of our Lord Jesus Christ, the Father of glory, may give you the Spirit of wisdom and of revelation in the knowledge of him, **having the eyes of your hearts enlightened,** that you may know what is the hope to which he has called you, what are the riches of his glorious inheritance in the saints, and what is the immeasurable greatness of his power **toward us who believe,** according to the working of his great might that he worked in Christ when he raised him from the dead and seated him at his right hand in the heavenly places,

Notice; The Apostle Paul is wanting Believers to open the eyes of your understanding of the world of the Spirit and know your calling and how to use your inheritance from Jesus Christ for the purposes GOD will show you.

The Apostle Paul is not talking about your eyes for vision in the natural but opening the eyes of your Born-again Spirit. To open the eyes of your Spirit and the world operating outside time, Believers must understand that the brain is in the present and will die with the body but the mind is part of your being that is eternal.

So, let us look into your mind and brain to understand their construction and try to decipher how to use the eyes of your understanding;
- Your body operates in miles per hour.
- Your brain dies with your body.
- Your mind, soul, and spirit are eternal.
- Your brain operates at speeds way above the speed of light.
- Your mind controls the brain and **operates outside time** at quantum speeds.
- Your brain has a platform of motivation; either; love from GOD for Believers or self-preservation for the unbeliever.
- Your spirit and mind are 98+ percent of your being, your brain is an organ in your body, and comprises just over 1% of your being.
- Your brain may receive from 50,000 to 200,000 or more thoughts from your cognitive functions daily.
- All of your body's cognitive functions; eyes, ears, nose, touch, taste, react to outside stimuli at quantum speeds above the

speed of light.

• Your mind controls your brain at faster speeds than reaction time to your cognitive functions.

• Your mind sweeps thoughts every 10 seconds and distributes them according to the motivational protocol of your spirit, either dead to GOD or Born-again (good to keep or evil to dispel).

• Your mind controls choices to store or expel all thoughts according to the foundational principle under which your "being" is operating.

• Your mind, with a foundation of GOD's love and peace, can make a jealous thought lay down in the peace of GOD's love until the mind expels it.

• Your mind **without** GOD and with a self-centered foundation **cannot** minister peace to a thought of jealousy or revenge because you have no controlling mechanism to bring the thought into captivity, it continues causing chaos and growing without closure.

• Your identity is determined by your choice to be a child of GOD or to be self-centered. The mind motivated by love can react to all stimuli without drama and chaos, because the reactions to stimuli are based in love and the actions are pre-programmed to be love, joy, goodness, patience, temperance, meekness, peace, and self-control.

• The self-centered mind has chaos in every decision because the thoughts governing reaction, have to be determined individually, without an underlying direction.

• For example: to the self-centered mind, if someone does something positive, the self-centered mind must decide if the action was positive or was it done with a deceitful motive. The self-centered life platform does not have a sea of forgiveness but operates on an avenue of get even.

• Your cognitive devices (eyes, etc.) are bringing billions

of bits of information every minute, what you're seeing, hearing, tasting, etc. and your brain is preparing to act on needs of the body,

- For example: if you are in a sandstorm your eyes will water and your eye lids will blink and restrict the opening to keep your eyes functioning at lightning speed.

- Your control of your thoughts is completely dependent on bringing every thought captive to the Lordship of Jesus Christ and allowing the Holy Spirit to council your mind regarding keeping thoughts or dispelling chaotic thoughts.

You are wonderfully and marvelously made as David said in Psalms 139:14. Consider the functioning of the eyes for the creative power resident in your brain and the need for the mind of Christ to control and use the brain;

Your eyes are driven by 130 million light sensitive receptor impulses to a photo chemical reaction that transforms light into electrical impulses that go to the brain to produce pictures of what you are seeing, many times faster than the speed of light.

Ears bring in sound material to ponder and react according to the instruction of the mind to the brain.

The brain does not have a filter, until the mind sets parameters for the brain that direct the thoughts. The brain plants every thought. A thought grows in the soil of the brain and a thought of chaos grows proteins that produce energy and cause dis-ease in the brain causing disfunction.

The **Believer's mind** is making decisions based on the platform of GOD's love and can capture and diffuse the thoughts of condemnation, shame, and guilt (chaos). The Believer must have enough knowledge of GOD and His Word to counter the chaos and override chaotic thoughts with the platform of Love from GOD. Every ten minutes the mind sweeps the brain for thoughts to reject or accept according to the knowledge of GOD based on good or evil. Listen to the way the Apostle Paul said it;

> 2nd Corinthians 10:4 For the weapons of our warfare are not of the flesh but have divine power to destroy strongholds. **We destroy arguments and every lofty opinion raised against the knowledge of God,** and take every thought captive to obey Christ,

The self-centered mind does not have mechanisms to dispel condemnation, shame and guilt (chaos) and is the reason for the proclivity to divorce at the first road block in a marriage.

> For example; The husband or wife who say they have grown apart and it cannot be fixed is dealing with chaos disrupting the minds ability to control thoughts. When Believers react according to emotions instead of GOD's word, they will not have a divine outcome. GOD made man, male and female He created them. Man and wife are meant to be one with GOD and each other, If GOD is part of their marriage any thought against their union is a lie. Your vow to GOD, "till death do you part" is not to be taken lightly and your marriage will fail only if GOD is not the center of your marriage.

The important question for Believers is; Is your identity with GOD Almighty? Do you know enough about GOD and his word for your mind to divide your thoughts into the thoughts to keep and make brain mindsets and thoughts to dispel before they make strongholds of doubt and unbelief?

Jesus is all "in" and all "for" Believers
We must imagine the greatness of our GOD,
Who died to send the Holy Spirit to Believers?

If you thought, that the time of Jesus on Earth in a human body was a great time of GOD, you have **not grasped** the greatness of the New Covenant time of Jesus sending the Holy Spirit to abide in Believers. Jesus was one man on Earth, but the Holy Spirit of Jesus Christ is in everyone who ask the Father to be baptized with the Holy Spirit. Jesus died, to give Believers the Holy Spirit.

Jesus gave Believers "His peace" and told believers, "do not worry or be afraid". Think about the word "disease", dis-ease is the opposite of peace. (John 14:27) GOD's peace is more powerful than disease, worry, or fear. Be "At-ease" not "Dis-eased"; words are powerful and need to be used correctly or stopped if they are **not** building up the Believer. This fact, from our Lord, gives your mind the ability to dispel the thoughts of stress leading to dis-ease and brain dysfunction because chaotic thoughts are not the product of the Lord's peace.

Abiding in the Lord and the Lord abiding inside Believers, is the desire of the Lord and His offer to Believers, who choose, to remain in the peace of Jesus Christ. (John 15:4) Most denominations believe that the Holy Spirit comes with salvation and some denominations believe you have to ask GOD for the Holy Spirit, **to be safe follow the scripture;**

> Luke 11:13 If ye then, being evil, know how to give good gifts unto your children: **how much more shall *your* heavenly Father give the Holy Spirit to them that ask him?**

It is our destiny to grow so close to GOD, that Believers live in **all** the grace available at the Cross. Remember, that GOD Almighty the creator of the world and creator of your body; lives inside you, **where is the logic that** GOD is happy living with you in sickness, poverty, and next to demons? The Creator of the Universe is abiding with Believers, **if you are not**

communicating with and abiding with the Holy Spirit, you are living in man-made power. Believers will have what they believe.

What is wrong with this picture and what is the TRUTH? Unfortunately, **what you believe is what you will experience!** Saying this another way; you will have what you believe because the mind is limited to the information in the brain as a mechanism for action. Most religious people are still worshiping GOD based on the old covenant **before the giving of the Holy Spirit and have not advanced to the new covenant of living with the Holy Spirit of Jesus Christ given to Believers to confirm your identity, as a child of GOD. The Holy Spirit is your comforter but not many live comforted because they do not have an intimate relationship with the Holy Spirit and do not listen to nor speak to the Holy Spirit.**

As Believers, abide in GOD and GOD abides in them, through the Holy Spirit, the Holy Spirit acts as the Believer's lifeline to the attributes of GOD, and Believers will be living the abundant life. The Apostle Paul gives Believers a picture how to prepare our mind to start our day and prepare for the world and its evil.

> Ephesians 6:16 In all circumstances take up the **shield of faith,** with which you can **extinguish all** the flaming darts of the evil one; and take the **helmet of salvation,** and **the sword of the Spirit, which is the word of God, praying at all times in the Spirit, with all prayer and supplication.**

And from Proverbs, the instructions for your thought life and its effect on your life;

> Proverbs 4:20 My son, **be attentive to my words;** incline your ear to my sayings. **Let them not escape from your sight;** keep them within your heart. For

they are **life** to those who **find them,** and **healing to all their flesh.** Keep your heart with all vigilance, for from it flow the springs of life. Put away from you crooked speech, and put devious talk far from you.

Notice; the Believer must be active, reading, listening, and finding the words and sayings of GOD, that when voiced will bring about the more abundant life and keep you healthy and plant brain mindsets for the mind to activate when needed to conquer evil.

Listen to the words Believers should expect to hear from the Holy Spirit as Believers request leadership for every moment of living. What is the language of the Holy Spirit in your life? The Kingdom of GOD is inside you and must be activated, guided, and protected from inside your mind. Here is a list of the word phrases, that with repetition these phrases become brain mindsets and, as you meditate, your mind can activate the power in each phrase. The Holy Spirit will speak to your heart in these faith-filled phrases;

"Cast your care on Jesus, for He cares for you",
        1st Peter 5:7
"Be anxious for nothing and in everything give thanks,
        Philippians 4:6
"Speak to that mountain and cast it into the sea",
        Matthew 21:21
"Draw near to GOD and He will draw near to you",
        James 4:8
"Present your bodies as a living sacrifice",
        Romans 12:1-2
"Be strong in the Lord and the power of His might",
        Ephesians 6:10

"Love GOD with all your heart, mind, strength
     Mark 12:30
"Love your neighbor as yourself",
     Luke 10:27
"Pray unceasingly",
     1st Thessalonians 5:17
"Think on these things, whatsoever are true, excellent, of good report, worthy of praise
     Philippians 4:8
"Giving thanks always for all things unto God",
     Ephesians 5:20
"These signs shall follow those who believe",
     Mark 16:17
"Do everything in word or deed, do all in the name of Jesus",
     Colossians 3:17
"Lay hands on the sick and they shall recover",
     Mark 16:18
"Let not your heart be troubled, don't let it be afraid",
     John 14:1,27
"Cast out devils",
     Matthew 10:8
"Take every thought captive",
     2nd Corinthians 10:5
"Ask, seek, and knock and you shall find and it shall be opened",
     Matthew 7:7
"Rejoice and Praise GOD",
     Luke 19:37
"Put on the whole armor of GOD",
     Ephesians 6:13
"Resist the enemy and he will flee",
     James 4:7
"Have faith and not doubt that what you say will come to pass",
     Mark 11:23

"Believe on Him, whom He hath sent",
John 6:29
"Raise the dead",
Matthew 10:8
"Anoint with oil and the prayer for healing will save the sick",
James 5:8
"Put on your new self",
Ephesians 4:24
"Be kind one to another",
Ephesians 4:32
"Forgive one another as Christ has forgiven you",
"Have faith in GOD",
Mark 11:22
"Be found in Him",
Philippians 3:9
"Be angry and not sin",
Ephesians 4:26
"Be sober minded",
1st Peter 1:13
"Don't love money, be content with what you have",
Hebrews 13:5
"Put off your old self",
Colossians 3:9
"Do not repay evil with evil",
Romans 12:21
"Abound to every good work",
2nd Corinthians 9:8
"Be strong in the Lord and the power of His might",
Ephesians 6:10
"My peace, I give you"
John 14:27

Notice; these phrases are **actions for the Believer to do**, <u>not
actions for GOD to do</u>. GOD will not answer a prayer for

something GOD has given you authority to do. These phrases and more, are admonitions you will hear from the voice of the Holy Spirit, inside you, when you ask the Holy Spirit for wisdom, direction, and planning. **Remember,** you are the hands and legs GOD has on earth to deliver answers to prayers, gifts of kindness, and to declare the Gospel of Jesus Christ to a dying world. Think about some of the phrases, "Be angry and sin not" if the Holy Spirit brings this phrase to your mind, it will immediately, help you capture a thought and keep an action of anger from happening. When Spirit directed faith filled words are used, the words will succeed in the good work they were sent to accomplish. Bad thoughts must be captured and dispelled to protect your brain from chaos and your brain can remain in the peace the Lord has given you.

Listen to what GOD thinks about words and their ability to accomplish their objective;

> Isaiah 55:9 For as the heavens are higher than the earth, **so are my ways higher than your ways and my thoughts than your thoughts.** "For as the rain and the snow come down from heaven and do not return there but water the earth, making it bring forth and sprout, giving seed to the sower and bread to the eater, so shall my word be that goes out from my mouth; **it shall not return to me empty, but it (My word) shall accomplish that which I purpose, and (My Word) shall succeed in the thing for which I sent it.**

The new era with the Holy Spirit is one of overcoming the world and its --chaos and problems, with the Word and peace of GOD and the power of faith filled words spoken for a GODly purpose. Believers do not have to pray GOD down from heaven because GOD **is also inside Believers** ready, confirming to our mind and brain, words of actions for good works and faith filled words of

GOD, to voice that will succeed in the thing for which they were sent.

Ask, and It Will Be Given

The scripture from Matthew 7:7 is the narrative to describe the action of the life of a Believer. The Lord wants Believers to rest in the victory of Jesus over the enemy but be active in the pursuit of good works GOD has for Believers to do.

> Matthew 7:7 Ask, and it shall be given you; seek, and ye shall find; knock, and it shall be opened unto you: For every one that asketh receiveth; and he that seeketh findeth; and to him that knocketh it shall be opened.

Are you ready to live in concert with the Holy Spirit and allow Him to orchestrate your actions to maintain GOD's will in everything you say or do? If you are ready; ask, seek, and knock. Constantly think about; how can Believers practice communicating with the Holy Spirit and how can we know the still small voice or the loud voice of the Holy Spirit? First we must be speaking to the Holy Spirit about everything;

> Step one; Constantly be thanking GOD for what you have, not what you want. See the beauty in the GOD's creation, the sunrise and sunset, the trees and flowers, your children and your spouse, your vocation, and many more of God's creations as your day continues.

> Step two; Constantly ask the Holy Spirit; what He has planned in acts of kindness for you to do today? A kind word for a co-worker, genuine interest in the wellbeing of a friend's family, a thoughtful card for your spouse or child, a prayer for someone in need, a gift to help someone with a monetary need.

> Step three; Constantly be aware of your circumstances and expect a word of knowledge from the Holy Spirit

for someone in your path today. Capture the moment, Stop and let your mind join the Holy Spirit for a word for your situation, and then act as the Spirit leads you. Step four; Touch everyone and impart heart felt love from GOD. In this PC world don't go overboard with hugs but shaking hands and using your other hand to make the sincere greeting more important and leave a silent blessing to everyone you meet or can touch and an uplifting word, out loud when possible. **Remember you have GOD Almighty inside you.**

The Holy Spirit is also there to guide you when a negative situation arises and to evaluate which part of the armor of GOD to activate. DO NOT allow your emotions to guide you into earthly actions, not motivated by love and the word of GOD. Everything you can touch, smell, taste, see, and hear are temporary but the motivations of your heart are forever.

2nd Corinthians 4:18 While we **look not** at the things which are seen, but (look) <u>at the things which are not</u> <u>seen</u>: for the things which are seen *are* temporal; but **the things which are not seen *are* eternal.**

Do not act from emotions, they are not the truth, whether they are pleasant or painful. Act from the knowledge of GOD that is eternal.

Believers must recognize
where the situations of life originate.

Can you imagine sickness, demons, and poverty being a part of the abundant life, given to you, by GOD Almighty in John 10:10?

John 10:10 …. I (Jesus) came that they may **have life** and have it **more abundantly.**

The Believer's mind must recognize each negative issue and activate a brain-mindset to thwart the particular evil thought with a spiritual promise from the victory Jesus won at the cross. Remember negative situations are temporary and are felt by our senses and the answers are all spiritual because the mind can operate outside time;

Life issues arise from **the curses of the law,**
Life issues arise from **persecutions from people,** and
Life issues arise from the **stealing, killing, and destroying of the devil.**

Recognition of how the enemy is attacking, will allow the Believer to choose the spiritual strategy to thwart the attack. The words of the New Covenant preclude calling GOD down from Heaven to deal with our problem; GOD has taken care of our problem and told us what to do, to continue the Lord's victory over anything we encounter. Each attack on Believer's is dealt with in a specific spiritual manner. The Believer's renewed mind filled with repetition of the knowledge of GOD added to the brains foundation of GOD's love is ready for action.

• **Actions to combat curses of sickness, depression, and poverty** with the truth from GOD's word, confirms to our mind that Believers have been redeemed from the curses of the law. Listen to the Apostle Paul declare the curses finished at the cross of Jesus Christ;

Galatians 3:13 **Christ redeemed us from the curse of the law by becoming a curse for us**—for it is written, "Cursed is everyone who is hanged on a tree"—so that in Christ Jesus the blessing of Abraham might come to the Gentiles, so that we might receive the promised Spirit through faith. (Only the blessings of Abraham and the Gift of the Holy Spirit remain, the curses are now a lie.) The curses are listed in Deuteronomy 28:16.

• **Actions to combat persecution** for your belief in Jesus Christ; set up a mechanism in your mind to recognize and dispel thoughts of being subject to the judgment of people with evil in their heart and replace the thoughts of condemnation with the truth of the Love of GOD for you. Listen to the Apostle Paul on victory over condemnation;

> Romans 12:16 Never be wise in your own sight. **Repay no one evil for evil, but give thought to do what is honorable in the sight of all.** If possible, so far as it depends on you, live peaceably with all. Beloved, never avenge yourselves, but leave it to the wrath of God, for it is written, "Vengeance is mine, I will repay, says the Lord." To the contrary, "if your enemy is hungry, feed him; if he is thirsty, give him something to drink; for by so doing you will heap burning coals on his head." Do not be overcome by evil, but overcome evil with good.

• **Actions to combat the devil,** who is bombarding Believers with thoughts of evil and lies. Believers must take every thought captive to the Lordship and victory of Jesus Christ and using the truth call on GODly brain mindsets. Listen and meditate on these scriptures;

> 1st John 4:4 that greater is He (Holy Spirit) who is inside Believers than the devil in the world;
>
> James 4:7 Submit yourselves therefore to God. **Resist the devil, and he will flee from you. Ephesians 6:13** Therefore **take up the whole armor of God,** that you may be able to withstand in the evil day, and **having done all, to stand firm.**

Part of the criteria of evaluating the Believer's situation is to know; who did what to whom? Or who or what is causing problems in your life, so that the mechanisms of the brain can be summoned by your mind of Christ to accept or thwart every thought or action?

**All the promises Believers have inherited
are 1990 years old.**

Believers must believe and receive the gift of the Holy Spirit and create a mindset in your brain of the Believer's salvation and its benefits. The inheritance of the saints must be appropriated by faith **from 1990 years ago or outside time.** Remember, the Believer's mind is an eternal part of your Spirit being. The mind of Christ given to Believers operates outside time and can build a mindset of salvation and all its benefits from 1990 years ago and continuing into the future forever. The mind tells the brain to set up a mindset of salvation and all its benefits and the brain grows this mindset to fruition through belief and the introduction of knowledge of GOD and meditation. Brain mindsets take 21 days of repetition to become solid. **The word of GOD was with Jesus at the creation of the world** and **now is with Believers** according to John 1:1-3 this concept is outside time, because it serves thousands of years with a living principle.

> In the beginning was the Word, and the Word was with God, and the Word was God. He was in the beginning with God. All things were made through him, and without him was not anything made that was made. John 1:1-3
> **Romans 5:1-2** Therefore being justified by faith, we have peace with God through our Lord Jesus Christ: **By whom also we have access by faith into this grace** wherein we stand, and rejoice in hope of the glory of God.

Important truth; The words of Jesus, the Holy Spirit, and the Spirit of Believers **operate outside time** and resurrection power is inside the believer looking for the opportunity to answer a prayer and bring glory to an Almighty GOD who lives outside time. If Believers never understand that their Spirit is eternal and is in a body that will die, it is virtually impossible to understand how to appropriate by faith, the grace of GOD, thousands of years old in earth terms. How do you explain to yourself that before a Believer was born their sins were forgiven and the lawlessness they commit tomorrow will not go to their account because of the sacrifice of Jesus at the cross?

Jesus left one commandment to follow;
Luke 10:27 And he answered,
> "You shall love the Lord your God with all your heart
> and with all your soul and
> with all your strength and
> with all your mind, and
> your neighbor as yourself."

Did Jesus really mean, love GOD with all our heart, mind, soul, strength, and our neighbor as ourselves? Believers cannot accomplish this love without developing and using the Spiritual world, because our GOD is a Spirit.

Here is a question? Does this mean love GOD **all the time?** Can't we live our life and come to GOD, when we think we need Him? The absurdity of this line of thinking is obvious, **but commitment to GOD is the problem of every Christian on the planet.** Jesus lived and was tempted as we are tempted, but never failed to focus on his destiny. Believers must focus on GOD and our destiny to be a steward of God's grace in everything we do, every moment of every day or be caught up in the evil of the day.

Where is the Believer's focus?

Jesus was never sick, depressed, infected with a demon, and he had an infinite supply of everything He needed; **not because He was GOD, but because he loved GOD with all his heart, mind, soul, strength, and loved His neighbor as Himself.** Very important do not miss this point read the last sentence again. Jesus lived the way he wants Believers to live; loving GOD and using the word of GOD and the Holy Spirit to guide us into all actions. For example;

> James 3:17 But the wisdom from above is first pure, then peaceable, gentle, open to reason, full of mercy and good fruits, impartial and sincere. And a harvest of righteousness is sown in peace by those who make peace.

Think about this; there are 10,080 minutes in a week and most Christians are in church for 80 minutes a week and in the world 10,000 minutes of the week. If a Believer does not have a more enduring relationship with GOD than the 80 minutes a week, the world will consume the Christians thoughts and actions and GOD will be left out, stifling the Christians ability to activate the promises of GOD given to Christians. If a Christian does not speak to the Holy Spirit often and discern our Savior, Creator, and Holy Friend, you will live outside the inheritance you have received from Jesus Christ, as if the inheritance did not happen and the result will be living without divine supply for your actions.

> The Believer's brain is operating every minute of every day just like the soil of the earth, growing any seed that is planted. If 10,000 out of 10,080 minutes of the week, you are living in the world with all of its stimuli and chaos, your brain will be filled with strongholds that are **not** based on the word of GOD and these strongholds

will keep your life in chaos. The bible refers to these mindsets as strongholds and connects them with lies and the enemy.

The focus of your time and your thoughts will determine what thoughts are planted in your brain and what if any good brain mindsets have been built for the mind to activate. The Believer's relationship with the Holy Spirit and your belief in GOD and his direction for your life, minute by minute, will declare the power of your witness.

Enough of the bad news, the good news for those who are consumed with a relationship with the God-head of the Universe; the inheritance given to you by Jesus Christ will allow you to live in standing as child of GOD. Remember; the Believer is the beneficiary of the promises of GOD, and joined by the Holy Spirit, the executor of your inheritance to reign in life as a Priest and King. You have heard that Jesus is **King of Kings and Lord of Lords,** but have you realized that Believers are the Kings and the Lords?

> Revelation 1:6 And hath made (Believers) us kings and priests unto God and his Father; to him be glory and dominion for ever and ever. Amen.
> Revelation 5:10 And hast made us unto our God kings and priests: and we shall reign on the earth.

Can you receive this word?

Notes

THE JOURNEY
TO DISCOVER
GOD.

CHAPTER 4

The Name of Jesus
is more than words used to end a prayer.

Words have invisible power to change the physical world. Believers can use words to love someone or to destroy someone. Why did GOD Almighty say, the Name of Jesus is the name above every name (word) that has ever been named? The name of Jesus is more powerful than any word in the human language. Remember, Believers are authorized dealers of the grace of GOD including the use of the Name of Jesus for the benefit of others. Consider the power "in the name of Jesus", in this next example of healing as a description of the **Believer's standing** in the world to use the name of Jesus.

The power of the Name of Jesus

> Acts 4:13 Now when they (Pharisees) saw the boldness of Peter and John, and perceived that they were unlearned and ignorant men, they (Pharisees) marveled; and they took knowledge of them (Peter and John), that they had been with Jesus. And **beholding the <u>man</u> which was healed standing with them,** they could say nothing against it (the miraculous healing). But when they had commanded them to go aside out of the council, they conferred among themselves, Saying, <u>What shall we do to these men</u>? for that **indeed a notable miracle hath been done by them *is* manifest to all them that dwell in Jerusalem;** and <u>we cannot deny *it*</u>. But that it spread no further among the people,

let us straitly threaten them, that they speak henceforth to no man **in this name**. And they called them, and **commanded them not to speak at all, nor teach "in the name of Jesus".**

Words and names have power resident in them from their creation by GOD; when a word is used with "the standing" in the Spiritual world of GOD for a Spiritual purpose, the word's power must be respected.

How to build brain mindsets

The Mind and Brain cooperate through meditation and memorization; it takes 21 days to set a brain mindset of a promise of GOD. The mind can activate brain mindsets for action dealing with the issues of life. If a Believer plants seed-thoughts of the power of the Name of Jesus, the mind will be able to draw upon the mindset of the name of Jesus and its power. The Believer's mind can activate salvation benefit mindsets that can override thoughts of doubt and condemnation. The declaration of the name of Jesus Christ is above or more powerful than the name of evil, cancer, depression, or the devil.

Listen to the description of the Name of Jesus by Isaiah;
> **His name shall be called "Wonderful Counselor", "Mighty GOD", "Everlasting Father", and the "Prince of Peace".**

When Jesus gave Believers, the Holy Spirit, Jesus did not send the Holy Spirit to Believers without the miracles, the heart of compassion, the healing power, the delivering power, favor, and gifts we cannot even imagine. Jesus has given Believers **standing** in the Kingdom of GOD to use the Name of Jesus and the authority to enforce the laws written in Believer's hearts by GOD.

Ephesians 3:19-20 and to know the love of Christ that surpasses knowledge, that you may be filled with all the fullness of God. Now to him who is able to do far more abundantly than all that we ask or think, **according to the power at work <u>within us.</u>**

The spiritual world changes the visible world through the powerful Believer's faith filled words and compassion for considering others more significantly than yourself. "The name of Jesus" is not the four words to use to end a prayer; the **Believer has standing** to change the world through a word from GOD spoken from a heart of love, in the Name of Jesus.

Start today right now;

> When an opportunity comes for a depressive thought, **stop,** <u>remember,</u> and ***<u>say out loud</u>*** "I am the righteousness of GOD in Christ" I will not accept that thought. 1st Corinthians 1:30 When anxiety creeps into your thoughts capture the thought and remember you **<u>have not</u>** been given the spirit of fear, but the spirit of love, power, and a sound mind. 2nd Timothy 5:7

GOD's grace and the sacrifice of Jesus was made 1,990 years ago, but the "I am" GOD is living inside you, **right now, with all the Lord's inheritance.** The inheritance from the sacrifice of Jesus Christ is owned by the Believer, it is yours right now, you have the standing of Jesus Christ in this world to use the inheritance and GOD's love for the power to act in this world. If owning the inheritance of Jesus Christ is a new concept to you, you must change your mind to a more positive realization of the timing of the gift of Salvation and its benefits.

Your brain may be filled with chaos and you may have to detox your brain with a massive dose of GOD's word and meditation to clear strongholds of doubt and bad thinking. Believers need to take hold of our inheritance (grace) in the sacrifice of Jesus Christ by faith and act on the word of GOD, without doubting or unbelief. Every deliverance of depression, or healing of the body, or salvation of a soul brings glory to our Savior and it is our good service to tell the world the good things of GOD.

Certainly, the Holy Spirit came to Believers with the plan of GOD and with these items from the inheritance given Believers from Jesus Christ:

The Lord's blood redeemed the Believer's sin,
    by His stripes Jesus has healed our diseases,
        on His shoulders He bore our sorrows and
        carried our griefs,
He was pierced for our transgressions,
    His body was bruised for our iniquities,
        He was punished to bring us peace, and
        He was made poor
    that we might become rich.
Isaiah 53. 2nd Corinthians 8:9
Confirming everything with multiple scriptures listen to David;
Psalms 103:1 Of David.
Bless the LORD, O my soul, and all that is within me,
    bless his holy name!
        Bless the LORD, O my soul, and
        forget not all his benefits,
        who forgives all your iniquity,
    who heals all your diseases,
        who redeems your life from the pit,
    who crowns you with steadfast love and mercy,
who satisfies you with good

so that your youth is renewed like the eagle's.

Let us continue the journey

Recap for the development of a relationship with the Holy Spirit;
Love GOD with all your heart, mind, soul, and strength,
all the time.
Believe GOD's word and set up mindsets in your brain,
by memorizing and meditation, specific areas of GOD's
word to counter bad thinking,
Believers must communicate with the Holy Spirit inside
themselves, Believers must recognize;
curses from the law,
persecutions from people, and the
stealing, killing, and destroying of the devil,
to know how to deal with those situations.

Believers using the word of GOD, images of faith in GOD, the power of the mind of GOD and direction from the Holy Spirit can discern between the spirit of evil and GOOD. Believers acting in faith considering others more significantly than themselves will have supply from GOD and divine outcomes.

Listen to the declaration of the **perfecting of the Saints by Jesus;**
Hebrews 10:11 And every priest (in the Temple) stands
daily at his service, offering repeatedly the same
sacrifices, which can never take away sins. **But when
Christ had offered for all time a single sacrifice for
sins, he sat down at the right hand of God,** waiting
from that time until his enemies should be made a
footstool for his feet. For by a single offering **he has
perfected for all time those who are being sanctified.**
And the Holy Spirit also bears witness to us; for after

saying, "This is the covenant that I **will make** with them after those days, declares the Lord: I **will put** my laws on their hearts, and write them on their minds," then he adds, "**I will remember** **their sins and their lawless** **deeds no more." Where there is forgiveness of these,** **there is no longer (needed) any offering for sin.** **John 14:27** Peace I leave with you; my peace (shalom, total well-being) I give to you. Not as the world gives do I give to you. Let not your hearts be troubled, neither let them be afraid.

Create an image of Jesus perfecting your Born-again Spirit **for ALL TIME, as a mindset in your brain and realize that** **GOD's Spirit is living inside you, with your perfect** **born-again Spirit.** If you think you have sinned after salvation you denigrate the power of the cross and the Lord's sacrifice and are believing a lie. Any thought of condemnation is prideful and says, "Your sin is more powerful than the salvation offered at the cross". Beware; lawless deeds will not be remembered by GOD but there are consequences for lawlessness to your life on earth, for example if you overeat or drink you will be fat or a drunk.

How can Christians flip their switch
from doubt to belief?

GOD gave Believers His peace, you either have GOD's peace or you have given your peace away, by **not** meditating on GOD's word about peace until it is a mindset, that is greater than doubt or fear. That sounds harsh, but is a reality, GOD's word is absolute and anything less than belief in what the word of GOD declares, will corrupt confidence in salvation and all its benefits. Believers who do not have the Lord's peace must examine themselves to evaluate why? As a Believer, your conscience is perfectly clean by the sacrifice of Jesus and there are no lawless deeds that need forgiveness, nor will there be, because Jesus paid for all sins; past, present, and future. If your conscience condemns you, you must **reassure your heart** and brain with promises of GOD, specific to your doubt. After an intimate time with GOD's word and GOD's love, you can "flip the switch" and believe GOD. Peace flows from a forgiven conscience and joy from the knowledge of your redemption.

Jesus died, to give Believers the Holy Spirit, to be the ever-present "I am" in the Believer's life. **The power in the names of our GOD; "I am" redemption, "I am" health, "I am" peace, "I am" provision, and more, are the Believer's possessions, right now.** Think about it, "I am" is in the present tense not two thousand years ago, but right now. Jesus is; the way, the truth, and the life, (John 14:6) starting when the Believer **flips the switch** and believes. When Believers believe these <u>verses</u> your mind can instruct the brain to call on a mindset of GOD's word stored in your heart and you will turn the Believers, "light of the life of Jesus Christ **on**" and the darkness of evil will leave. Don't be confused: your body and bad habits leave at a slower pace than **your sin nature,** which leaves when you put GOD on the throne of your life and are born-again. The darkness of your sin nature leaves your Spirit instantly.

Ask yourself, am I "all in with GOD" or "my marriage", or "my children" or anything other than myself? The Believer who **will not grow** their knowledge of GOD and His promises, **will not have** mindsets in the brain for the mind to draw from to activate the Lord's victory. **Remember;** there are 10,080 minutes in a week, and you spend how many of those minutes storing good mindsets of GOD's word in your brain and how many minutes storing strongholds of the lust of the world and the influence of the devil? When faith is taken away from grace, the manifestation of GOD's supply will **not** be available, and Believers will flounder.

> Doubters are captive to condemnation by their conscience, believing they are not worthy of GOD's blessing because they do not believe they are forgiven every transgression. Condemnation creates chaos in your brain because there are competing philosophies of motivation. This is the reason the Lord said, "Don't' be double minded". James 1:8

Many Christians believe they are only forgiven until they were saved, and after salvation, they are condemned for their present sins, without realizing the power of the salvation of Jesus Christ. **This condemnation is not logical, because Jesus died for your sins 1990 years ago, all of the Believer's sins were in the future when Jesus forgave them.** Believers must believe their name was written in the "Lamb's Book of Life" and act on their belief to marry the grace of GOD with the faith of the Believer and compassion for others.

> **Romans 5:1** Therefore being justified **by faith, we have peace** with God through our Lord Jesus Christ: By whom also we have access **by faith into this grace** wherein we stand and rejoice in hope of the glory of God. For by **grace you have been saved through faith.** And this is not your own doing; it is the gift of God, not a result of works, so that no one may boast.

There is now, no condemnation for those in Christ Jesus. (Romans 8:1) **Grace is not based on the Believer's actions but based on GOD's love.** Grace is GOD's part of divine action added to the faith of the Believer. A combination of grace, faith, and communication with the Holy Spirit will propel victory to get through or over any and all situations that are considered problems by Believers. The focus can't be on you and your need but on GOD and His provision. **Remember, if your actions**

were not part of prayer or meeting with the Holy Spirit to plan your day, you do not have a path for a divine outcome and supply from GOD.

Foundational truth.

You cannot be the god of your world and occasionally ask the **GOD of the Universe** to help you with a problem you have created with faith in yourself. **Read that again,** do you understand, you can't be the god of your world and occasionally ask **the GOD of the Universe** to save you from a situation you're in because you are not leaning on GOD for your understanding? If there is no faith in your actions and therefore no grace from GOD available; you are acting on a man-made plan and you will have a man-made result.

What kind of soil is in your <u>heart</u>
And what kind of thoughts are in your brain?

Listen to the explanation of Jesus, as He tells Believers, about the secret of the Kingdom of GOD. Jesus reveals the four kinds of soil in mankind's heart or seed-thoughts coming to the Believer's brain. Think about it; A convert may be a Christian, but the soil in a sometime Christian's heart may not be good soil and the seed of GOD's word is subject to the growth and harvest revealed by the type of soil in your heart. The soil in your heart can be energized by spending time with the Lord and adding the word of GOD into your heart. Think about the word "Heart", it is composed of ear, hear, and art; the emphasis is on the art of hearing from the Holy Spirit.

Matthew 13:13 This is why I speak to them in parables, because seeing they do not see, and hearing they do not hear, nor do they understand. Indeed, in their case the prophecy of Isaiah is fulfilled that says: You will indeed hear but never understand, and you will indeed see but never perceive." **For this people's heart has grown dull, and with their ears they can barely hear, and their eyes they have closed, lest they should see with their eyes and hear with their ears and understand with their heart and turn, <u>and I would heal them.</u>'** But blessed are your eyes, for they see, and your ears, for they hear. For truly, I say to you, many prophets and righteous people longed to see what you see, and did not see it, and to hear what you hear, and did not hear it.

The question for all Believers is, "has our heart grown dull and are we not hearing or seeing and understanding with our hearts, <u>the correct path to total-wellbeing by Jesus Christ?</u>"

Mark 4:10 And when he was alone, those around him with the twelve asked him about the parables. Jesus now, elaborated on **the secret to the Kingdom of God** which is inside Believers.

In the modern day, with a society not built on agriculture, substitute the Brain for the soil and use the keys to the kingdom of GOD to build a picture of good and evil thoughts in your brain and how to develop brain mindsets and controlling your thought life, dispelling strongholds of doubt.

And Jesus said to them,

"To you has been given the secret of the kingdom of God,

but for those outside everything is in parables,
so that "they may indeed see
but not perceive,
and may indeed hear but not understand,
lest they should turn (repent)
and be forgiven."

And he said to them, "Do you not understand **this** parable?

How then will you understand all the parables?
The sower sows the word.
And these are the ones along the path,
where the word is sown:
When they hear,
Satan immediately comes and
takes away the word that is sown in them.
And these are the ones sown on rocky ground:
the ones who, when they hear the word,
immediately receive it with joy.
And they have no root in themselves,
but endure for a while; then,
when tribulation or persecution arises
on account of the word,
immediately they fall away.
And others are the ones sown among thorns.
They are those who hear the word,
but the cares of the world and
the deceitfulness of riches and the
desires for other things
enter in and choke the word,
and it proves unfruitful.
But those that were sown on the good soil
are the ones who hear the word
and accept it and bear fruit,
thirtyfold and
sixtyfold and
a hundredfold."

The Lord's explanation reveals the problems, all Christians face, according to the condition of the Believer's heart. Jesus tells us that our lives **will be** and **are based** on the amount of GOD's word **we believe** and act on. If you study each picture you see the areas of belief in the word of GOD;

Satan steals much of the word of GOD in your heart, Persecution and tribulation drive the faint of heart away.

The pursuit of riches diverts the doubters from following GOD.

Even the Believers with good soil have levels of belief and doubt, that affect their ability to use the word of GOD to bring glory to Jesus and Father GOD.

This chapter from Mark 4 is a picture of integration of your mind and brain to set up brain mindsets, that the mind can activate, energize, and send actions to parts of your life for performance. This is the secret to the Kingdom of GOD, only the Believers who love GOD and believe the seed of GOD's word will produce fruit and plant GOD's word in your brain, <u>will have the divine result</u>. Listen to Gospel of Mark

Mark 4:26-28 And he said, "The kingdom of God is as if a man should scatter seed on the ground. He sleeps and rises night and day, **and the seed sprouts and grows; he knows not how. The earth produces by itself,** first the blade, then the ear, then the full grain in the ear.

Your mind and brain will grow knowledge of GOD and your harvest will be righteousness of good deeds that bring glory to GOD.

Remember from Genesis 1; The GOD (Elohim, the word for the plural GOD) spoke to the ground to bring forth grass and seed bearing trees and herbs, then GOD spoke to the earth to bring forth animals and every living creature, then GOD spoke to the seas to bring forth sea creatures and the flying creatures. **Everything was already in the soil and the water that GOD had made waiting on GOD to speak life.** In the same way, The

New Creation brain will grow any seed you plant in your brain; seeds of life, seeds of prosperity and good health. The picture given Believers, by GOD, is to speak to the mind to bring forth from the seeds planted and nurtured that you have put into your soil of your brain.

Listen to the theme of the Apostle Paul in Romans 12 and realize that renewing your mind is returning the mind, to the creation example when its foundation was love. Believers are part of GOD and **GOD is love and there is no fear in love.** These truths are outside time, but in control of the mind of Christ, given to Believers.

Romans 12:1 present your bodies as a living sacrifice, holy and acceptable to God, which is your spiritual worship. **Do not be conformed to this world, but be transformed by the renewal of your mind,** that by testing you may discern what is the will of God, And **be not** conformed to this world: but be ye transformed by the renewing of your mind, that ye may prove what *is* that **good, and acceptable, and perfect, will of God.**
what is good (Thirty fold)
     and acceptable (Sixty fold)
          and perfect will of GOD. (One hundred-fold)

Notice the levels of the pursuit of God's will and the product of the good soil are aligned.

Do you understand how a thought matures to the Believer's destiny?

A Believer's underlying motivation (love, joy, peace, et cetera) leads to **decisions,**
Decisions based on your motivation lead to **actions,**
Actions based on decisions, motivated by GOD, and meditated

on will develop **habits**,

Habits based on actions, directed by decisions, motivated by GOD and His word, build **character.**

Character based on habits, of actions directed by decisions, motivated by GOD and His word, will find the Believer, at a GOD planned **destination.**

Destination motivated by a plan of GOD, directed by decided actions, producing habits, developed in to character, will deliver you to your **destiny.**

Do you understand how thoughts mature to death and destruction?

An unbeliever or doubter's **emotions** (anger, greed, revenge, and self-centeredness) lead to decisions,

Decisions based on sense driven emotions, lead to **actions,**

Actions based on emotions and providing for yourself, without GOD, are motivated by **selfishness.**

Selfishness based emotions and provision by yourself, without GOD, leads to actions laced with **fear.**

Fear motivated actions, have no respect for others, and produce **hate.**

Hate filled hearts based on fear, make decisions that lead to the destruction of yourself; produce unhappiness, and end in **death.**

**Are you in the situation you're <u>in</u>,
because you did not ask GOD for direction
before you acted.**

Do you default into calling for GOD to come down from Heaven to die on the cross again, because you do not have enough knowledge of GOD and His promises to speak life to your situation? What do you think Jesus meant when He said that "It is finished.'"? And have you received the Holy Spirit the Lord offered to Believers. At the first sign of a problem, do you analyze it according to GOD's word or do you react as if your ability is the only answer. Before Believers react to any situation, we should examine the underlying cause of the problem to understand the Holy Spirit's direction to solve the problem.

Believers' first choice should be to call on the power of God inside you and act in concert with the Holy Spirit. What do you do, when you hear; a rejection from a friend, a symptom of sickness from the doctor, or a disruption notice from the electric company? This life issue is an opportunity to see what kind of soil is in your heart or your brain mindsets;

> When you heard the word on provision, healing, and deliverance; did Satan come by and steal that word from your heart?
> Or did the word of healing, deliverance, and more; land on a rocky part of your heart and not take root?
> Or did the persecution of your belief in the miracles of the cross cause your friends to make fun and you abandoned your faith?
> Or did the deceitfulness of riches and desire to be part of the "in crowd" choke the word of GOD and make the word unfruitful?
> Or did your church not teach you that the Holy Spirit inside Believers is your power to reign in life and consequently you are still trying to get GOD to come down from Heaven to die on the cross for your problem?
> **Or did you take a stand on the word of GOD and order your mind to call on a brain mindset and reply with I am the righteousness of GOD in Jesus Christ and nothing formed against me can prosper, and greater is the Holy Spirit that is in me than the enemy that is in the world.**

GOD wants to be your ever-present help in a time of need with the grace stored up for you from the Cross. Any **consequence in your life** that comes from you following the desires of your flesh instead of the leading of the Holy Spirit is a dilemma. The Believer and GOD need to be on the same page. For example, Abraham, when he slept with the maid-servant Hagar and produced a son out of adultery, that was not GOD's plan, and Abraham's family and the world suffered the consequence of his action. There are consequences to actions that keep Believers in their circumstances instead of their inherited victory. Character is more important than expediency.

> **Remember; Believers are not in a religion**
> **but in a relationship with a living GOD.**
> **What is your relationship with GOD like?**

In the present religious world, preachers and teachers teach, "Believe on Jesus and your sins are forgiven" this teaching requires no objective proof or change in seekers life revealing a change from receiving salvation. What does "believe on Jesus" and you will be saved include? Look at this scripture about the Holy Spirit confirming the sacrifice Jesus made for Believers;

> **1st John 5:6** Jesus Christ is the one who came. He came with water and with blood. He did not come by water only. No, Jesus came by both water and blood. And the Spirit tells us that this is true. The Spirit is the truth. So there are **three witnesses** that tell us about Jesus: the **Spirit**, the **water**, and the **blood**. **These three witnesses agree.**

Your seal of the inheritance of Jesus Christ is the Holy Spirit to be in and on Believers, who ask GOD for the Holy Spirit. Believers must believe; that the works based old covenant of the Ten Commandments is obsolete and has been fulfilled by Jesus

Christ. The New Covenant of GOD Almighty made with Jesus Christ; has been obtained through His death and resurrection, and is the inheritance of Believers.

Listen and take to heart the words of Almighty GOD;
> Hebrews 8:10 For this is the covenant that **I will** make with the house of Israel after those days, declares the Lord: **I will** put my laws into their minds, and write them on their hearts, and **I will** be their God, and they shall be my people. Hebrews 8:12 For **I will** be merciful toward their iniquities, and **I will** remember their sins no more." In speaking of a new covenant, he (Jesus) makes the first one obsolete.

Jesus died to give Believers the Holy Spirit to be GOD with you and write on your heart GOD's instructions and be your GOD. Again the job of the Believer is to believe that GOD will be merciful to your iniquities and will remember your sins no more, and be your GOD. The new covenant is the new foundation of GOD in the world; the foundation replaces the sin nature and installs the love of GOD in your brain, NOW, the motivation for your mind to react to the issues of life, can be in concert with the Holy Spirit.

> 2nd Corinthians 3:4 **Such is the confidence that we have through Christ toward God.** Not that we are sufficient in ourselves to claim anything as coming from us, **but our sufficiency is from God, who has made us sufficient to be ministers of a new covenant,** not of the letter but of the Spirit. For the letter kills, but the Spirit gives life.

America, in its inception, was a place to worship GOD and now is more a place to worship success. GOD's promise is Love GOD with all your heart, strength, mind, and your neighbor as yourself and GOD will supply all your needs. This does not mean quit your job, it means lean not unto your own understanding but lean on the knowledge of GOD and GOD will direct your paths. Change your thinking.

Rules of thinking.
• You can't believe **beyond** what you know. Your mind cannot operate on information, the mind does not have, and is not able to be reflexive.
• What you are focused on will dominate you and what you do not focus on will not be active in your life.
• What you do, does not consider, what will not happen.

Is your focus; the supernatural laws of GOD or the natural laws of man.

Listen to these Bible situations;
Abraham **considered not** his own body nor the deadness of Sarah's womb, but believed GOD. (right thinking)

Sarai **considered her body as barren and doubted GOD** and took Hagar and gave her to Abram and they had a child. (wrong thinking)

Eve was not tempted to eat of the tree of the knowledge of good and evil **for years and years** and then the devil told her she could be like GOD and **she considered the tree and hardened her heart to what GOD had declared.** Eve acted on her thought and **took what was not hers to take** and Adam and Eve suffered along with the entire world.

The Disciples, all saw (Jesus walking on the water) him and were troubled. And immediately he (Jesus) talked with them, and saith unto them, Be of good cheer: it is I; be not afraid. And he went up unto them into the ship; and the wind ceased: and they were sore amazed in themselves beyond measure, and wondered. For they **considered not** the miracle of the loaves: **for their heart was hardened.** Mark 6:50 The walking on the water was just hours later from the feeding of the multitude, and the disciples were amazed at Jesus speaking to the wind to be still. **What were they thinking?**

The brain is damaged by bad thoughts, that set up strongholds, that produce proteins, that have energy and cause chaos; which causes the brain to be dis-eased with dysfunction. In the medical world; When the brain is not working correctly, the answer is to add chemicals, but medicine is not good for the brain. Depression is a not a disease but a disfunction of the brain that can be fixed with proper thought. **Remember,** dis-ease for the brain causes all the brain disfunctions, because the thoughts in the brain are not at-ease or at peace but instead are like an electric cord with nothing on the open end just sparking and jumping around without purpose.

The Healing Ministry of Jesus Christ

Believers cannot deny that a main part of the Ministry of Jesus Christ was the healing of those with infirmities, demons, and sicknesses and those oppressed of the devil. Consider these next verses, to clarify the mission of Jesus included: healing the sick, delivering the depressed, casting out demons, and raising the dead? Jesus is the same forever, and only did what He saw the Father do, and Jesus has given those who ask the same Holy Spirit he was baptized with for power in His ministry; how can we deny that total well-being is not part of Salvation? Listen and meditate on the following scriptures;

Hebrews 13:8 Jesus Christ is the same yesterday and

today and forever.

John 5:19 So Jesus said to them, "Truly, truly, I say to you, the Son can do nothing of his own accord, but only what he sees the Father doing. For whatever the Father does, that the Son does likewise.

Acts 10:38 how God anointed Jesus of Nazareth **with the Holy Spirit and with power.** He went about doing good and **healing all** who were oppressed by the devil, for God was with him.

Meditate on this scripture; If Jesus was not on earth as a man, "why did GOD anoint Jesus with power and the Holy Spirit at his baptism, before Jesus had done one miracle. If Jesus needed the Holy Spirit and power, can it be any different for Believers to need the Holy Spirit and power.

The Bible details the Lord's miracle healings 48 times. Everywhere he went, the Lord healed individuals or small groups but 17 of these times the Bible reports Jesus "healed all". The description of the size of the groups is mind-blowing; the descriptions are: Cities and villages brought the sick and laid them in the street, multitudes followed Him and he healed them all, many were healed and many were delivered and many were set free describing one event, and more. Listen to what the Apostle John said about the ministry of Jesus Christ;

John 21:25 And there are also many other things which Jesus did, the which, if they should be written every one, **I suppose that even the world itself could not contain the books that should be written.** Amen.

Can you imagine the magnitude of this scripture, the world **could not hold** the books of the healings and other good things the

Lord did on the earth? Explore these scriptures to realize the compassion of the Lord's heart. **Take note:** Jesus did not do one miracle or healing in His ministry until He was baptized with the Holy Spirit at His baptism? Can you picture the standing in the world, that being baptized with the Holy Spirit means to the power in your life as a Believer? Below are all the healings in the New Testament. Jesus told Believers, He was the way, the truth, and the life; and later told Believers He would send the Spirit of truth, to be inside Believers. The Spirit came with resurrection power according to the Apostle Paul, so that we can have confidence to act with power to be a steward of GOD's power to do good. If your church teaches that you received the Holy Spirit at salvation, but you are not realizing an intimate relationship with the person of the Holy Spirit, ASK GOD right now to give you an expanded relationship with the Holy Spirit and in faith start communication, today right now?

The multitudes followed Him and he healed them all.

In Matthew	In Mark	In Luke	In John
4:23-24	1:32-34	4:40	
8:16-17	1:39	6:17-19	
9:35	6:56	7:21	
12:15		9:11	
14:14		17:12-17	
14:34-36			
15:30-31			
19:2			
21:14			

The Lord healed individuals and small groups in these scriptures;

In Matthew	In Mark	In Luke	In John
8:1-15	1:40-45	4:33-39	4:46-54
8:28-34	2:1-12	5:12-15	5:2-15
9:1-8	3:1-5	5:17-26	9:6-7
9:20-33	5:1-20	6:6-10	11:43-44
12:10-13	5:25-43	7:1-17	
	7:24-37	8:27-39	
	8:22-26	8:43-56	
	9:14-29	9:37-42	
	10:46-52	11:14	
		13:11-17	
		14:1-5	
		18:35-43	
		22:50-51	

Jesus left Believers a legacy of redemption, healings, deliverances, miracles and a prophecy of greater works than Jesus did, shall Believers do, because Jesus is going to the Father and sending the Holy Spirit to be in and on Believers.

> John 14:10 Do you not believe that I am in the Father and the Father Is in me? The words that I say to you I do not speak on my own authority, but the Father who dwells in me does his works. Believe me that I am in the Father and the Father is in me, or else believe on account of the works themselves. **"Truly, truly, I say to you, whoever believes in me will also do the works that I do; and greater works than these will he do, because I am going to the Father.** Whatever you ask in my name, this I will do, that the Father may be glorified in the Son. If you ask me anything in my name, I will do it.

Conclusion:

Imagine this conversation with Jesus at the right hand of GOD talking to Father GOD when GOD hears a cry for salvation, healing, deliverance or lack.

GOD speaking to Jesus,
Did you not tell the Believers you have already been to the cross for their salvation and all its benefits and all they have to do is believe in your death and resurrection to receive the benefits?

Jesus said, I told them over and over,
Believers seem to be saying, they want us to do for them, "what we have already done for them".

GOD saying, I had Peter tell them, they **were healed** in the past tense.

Jesus saying, I know, I had Paul tell Believers, not to be condemned; that there was nothing that could separate Believers from us and our love for them.

GOD saying, I sent Believers, who ask, the same Holy Spirit, I sent to you, when you were on the earth.

Jesus speaking, I know, I had Paul tell Believers, the immeasurable greatness of the Holy Spirit power toward those who believe, according to the working of his great might that you worked in Me when you raised Me from the dead and seated Me here at your right hand in the heavenly places, far above all rule and authority and power and dominion, and above every name that is named, not only in this age but also in the one to come.

GOD speaking, Why are they still coming to us instead of believing they already have what they need for life and godliness?

Isaiah 26:3 You keep him in **perfect peace** whose **mind is stayed on you,** because he trusts in you.

Notes

CHAPTER 5

**A few drops of Jesus blood
were sufficient to save the world.
What was the purpose for
the scourging of the body of Jesus Christ?**

**The Blood necessary for total redemption of the world could
have been accomplished with a few drops of blood from the
little finger of Jesus Christ. Why was the body of Jesus put
through the terrible scourging, crushing, beating,
humiliation, etc.** Redemption for mankind, only needed sinless
blood, it did not need a painful death. **At the Temple,** the
sacrifice for sin was a lamb without spot or blemish, not a lamb
beaten within a minute of its death. **Where is the logic for the
scourging of the Lord's body?**

The body of our Lord suffered every conceivable calamity of
mankind, so that mankind can choose **to cast any care** (life
issue) on Jesus to carry (eradicate). GOD had a reason for the
horrific death of our Savior and at the last supper, Jesus gave
Believers a clue in the Communion Observance. Salvation and
the new covenant are evidenced by the wine. The bread
represents the body of Jesus Christ broken and given for
Believers in the Lord's Supper.

Take a fresh look at Communion; Communion is worship to our
Lord and is the picture of the Lord caring for mankind. Believers
should have communion as often as needed to keep Jesus in the
center of your remembrance, do not wait for the celebration of

Communion at church. Listen to the Apostle Paul talk about communion and the importance of Believer's imagination of the Lord's body in the crucifixion and resurrection;

> 1st Corinthians 11:28 Let a person examine himself, then, and so eat of the bread and drink of the cup. For anyone who eats and drinks **without discerning the body (Jesus Christ) eats and drinks judgment on himself.** That is why many of you are **weak and ill, and some have died**.

"The question is" are believers **discerning the Body and blood of Jesus sacrificed for you** and if Believers do not understand right-standing with GOD and the total wellbeing of our bodies from the cross, **that ignorance or unbelief** causes people **to be weak, sick, and die. Believing in Jesus Christ and the total-wellbeing available from his sacrifice is paramount for living the abundant life given Believers through Jesus Christ**.

What do you believe, when you read this verse from 1st Corinthians?

The Communion acknowledgment should be experienced as often as a Believer's focus on Jesus has dimmed. The blessing of your daily meals is an opportunity to remember the Lord, not just a thought without substance but capturing a moment to remember Jesus Christ and His love for each Believer. Everything in our world was made and is controlled by the Lord Jesus Christ including the Believer's inheritance. Remember Jesus, said **"do this in remembrance of me"**. Expect to be **healed and blessed** each time we lift up the broken body of Jesus Christ sacrificed for your peace and total wellbeing when breaking bread and celebrating the cup. And if **Believers do not lift up the Lord** and remember his sacrifice and love for Believers; expect to be sick, weak, and die.

In the sermon detailing the Bread of Life in John 6 the Lord stresses the importance of understanding the love expressed by the willing sacrifice of GOD through the body of Jesus Christ for Believers.

> John 6:53 So Jesus said to them, "Truly, truly, I say to you, unless you eat the flesh of the Son of Man and drink his blood, **you have no life in you.** Whoever feeds (constantly eating and drinking) on my flesh and drinks my blood has eternal life, and I will raise him up on the last day. For my flesh is true food, and my blood is true drink. **Whoever feeds on my flesh and drinks my blood abides in me, and I in him.** As the living Father sent me, and I live because of the Father, **so whoever feeds on me, he also will live because of me. This is the bread that came down from heaven, not like the bread the fathers ate, and died. Whoever feeds on this bread will live forever."**

Notice; **Whoever feeds (continually) on my flesh and drinks my blood, abides in me and I in him and will live forever.**

For emphasis of the importance of breaking of bread; Listen to the first gospel record of Jesus during the <u>forty days after resurrection,</u> after his first ascension to heaven; Notice there is no wine, representing redemption from sin.

Soon after Jesus ascended to heaven for the delivery of the First Fruits Offering of His blood and the Saints who were resurrected when he was resurrected (Matthew 27:51), the Lord returned to earth and met the two disciples on the road to Emmaus. **Imagine,** Jesus, after returning from Heaven, He met two disciples on the road to Emmaus, a small village seven miles from Jerusalem. Do you have this picture in your mind, Imagine the setting, what do the holes in the Lord's hands and feet look like, after resurrection, what is Jesus wearing, as they walk to Emmaus and why don't the disciples recognize Him immediately?

Jesus has ascended to Heaven with the First Fruits offering and next appeared to the two disciples on the road to Emmaus.

Luke 24:13 That very day two of them were going to a village named Emmaus, about seven miles from Jerusalem, and they were talking with each other about all these things that had happened. While they were talking and discussing together, **Jesus himself drew near** and went with them. But their eyes were kept from recognizing him. And he said to them, "What is this conversation that you are holding with each other as you walk?" And they stood still, looking sad. Then one of them, named Cleopas, answered him, **"Are you the only visitor to Jerusalem who does not know the things that have happened there in these days?"** And he said to them, "What things?" And they said to him, "Concerning Jesus of Nazareth, a man who was a prophet mighty in deed and word before God and all the people, and how our chief priests and rulers delivered him up to be condemned to death and crucified him. But we had hoped that he was the one to redeem Israel. Yes, and besides all this, it is now the third day since these things happened. Moreover, some women of our company amazed us. They were at the tomb early in the morning, and when they did not find his body, they came back saying that they had even seen a vision of angels, who said that he was alive. Some of those who were with us went to the tomb and found it just as the women had said, but him they did not see." And he said to them, **"O foolish ones, and slow of heart to believe all that the prophets have spoken! Was it not**

**necessary that the Christ should suffer these things
and enter into his glory?"** And beginning with Moses
and all the Prophets, he interpreted to them in all the
Scriptures the things concerning himself. So they drew
near to the village to which they were going. He acted
as if he were going farther, but they urged him strongly,
saying, "Stay with us, for it is toward evening and the
day is now far spent." So he went in to stay with them.

Now Jesus reveals the reason for the bread in communion and the
power of revelation of Jesus body in the Spirit world by the
breaking of bread;

Luke 24:30 When he was at table with them, he took
the bread and blessed and broke it and gave it to them.
**And their eyes were opened, and they recognized
him. (epi nosis, complete knowledge)**

Take a minute; Think about Adam and Eve, they ate the
forbidden fruit and their eyes were opened and knew **they were
naked.** The disciples on the road to Emmaus, after the blessing
and breaking of the bread and the remembrance of Jesus, **their
eyes were opened, and they saw into the Spiritual world, they
saw the risen Christ and they recognized Him** (were intimate
with Him).

And he vanished from their sight. They said to each
other, "Did not our heart (one heart, the disciples were
most likely a married couple) burn within us while he
talked to us on the road, while he opened to us the
Scriptures?" And they rose that same hour and returned
to Jerusalem. And they found the eleven and those who
were with them gathered together, saying, "The Lord
has risen indeed, and has appeared to Simon!" (Then
the two from the road to Emmaus) they told what had
happened on the road, **and how he was known to**

them in the breaking of the bread.

Believers must not miss the power of the Communion observance and do not just celebrate it at Church but celebrate the victory of Jesus Christ with communion at home, at work, or at the Hospital. Celebrate often to visualize the sacrifice of the Lord's body and blood and to point your family to the Father GOD to always be in remembrance of Jesus. Listen to what Jesus said about visualizing his image at the cross;

> John 3:14-15 And as Moses lifted up the serpent in the wilderness, so must the Son of Man be lifted up, that whoever believes in him may have eternal life.

When the brass image of a serpent was held up by Moses everyone that looked upon the image, who had been bitten by the poison snakes **was healed.** It is the lifting up of Jesus Christ that brings salvation and total well-being to those who discern the Lords body, given for the world. The next verse is John 3:16.

Circumstances and opportunities

Again, I say, **a Believer indwelt with the Holy Spirit is an authorized dealer of the manifestation of God's grace and has authority to enforce laws written in your heart by GOD.** All of the promises of Jesus Christ are "yes and amen" **to the Believer walking in love and considering others more significantly than ourselves.** Think about this; If you don't tell anyone about your testimony, of what GOD has done in your life, no one will get saved from your testimony and the Lord Jesus Christ will not be glorified. If you don't ever pray for or speak "life" to the sick or depressed, you will never see God's grace heal through the Name of Jesus and the Lord Jesus Christ will not be glorified and someone will remain sick until God sends another steward. Do not let anyone tell you that miracles are over, miracles are only over for those who don't believe. If miracles are over you can't be saved, **for surely salvation is a miracle.**

> Healing for others is mysterious and is at the will of the Holy Spirit and concerns individual choices and faith. Believers must not let the mystery of the Spiritual world, be a cover for the doubt of Believers to believe in resurrection power and the promise of scripture. Believers must constantly speak the Word of GOD over every heart felt motivation to pray for, speak to, anoint with oil, or lay hands on the unbelievers or Believers who are sick, depressed, or need salvation.

Where is the logic, **to <u>not</u> speak life to any and every situation?** GOD created the world and our bodies, and we are born-again of GOD's Spirit. GOD said, "Speak to those things that be not, as though they were." **If you do not speak to situations the way GOD designed them, you will have the situations the way they are.**

> Romans 4:17 before him whom he believed, even God, who quickeneth the dead, and calleth those things which be not as though they were.

Remember, GOD was in the darkness when He said, "Let there be light" and Jesus was in the midst of a great storm when He said, "Wind be still" and Peter and Paul said, to the lame man at the Gate Beautiful, "Silver and gold have we none but such as we have we give to you, Rise up and walk". And **GOD is the same yesterday, today, and forever and God is not a respecter of persons. The same Holy Spirit in Jesus, Peter, and Paul is in Believers, who ask.**

The Lord's words to Believers declare, **that Believers will do greater works than Jesus did because he is going to Heaven** and sending the **Holy Spirit to be in all Believers who ask.** (John 14:12). The religious hierarchy believe in the great <u>miracle of salvation,</u> **which you can't see,** but have problems believing for a visible miracle of healing, prosperity, or deliverance. Listen to Jesus, who addresses this problem in Matthew 9:5, Mark 2:9 and Luke;

> Luke 5:20 And when he saw their faith (the Pharisees watching), he said unto him, Man, thy sins are forgiven thee. And the scribes and the Pharisees began to reason, saying, *Who is this which speaketh blasphemies?* Who can forgive sins, but God alone?
> But when Jesus perceived their thoughts, he answering said unto them, What reason ye in your heart? **Whether is easier, to say, Thy sins be forgiven thee; or to say, Rise up and walk?** But that ye may know that the **Son of man** hath power upon earth to forgive sins, (he said unto the sick of the palsy,) **I say unto thee, Arise, and take up thy couch, and go into thine house.**
> And immediately he rose up before them, and took up that whereon he lay, and departed to his own house, glorifying God. **And they were all amazed, and they glorified God,** <u>and (the Pharisees) were filled with fear, saying, We have seen strange things today.</u>

Healing and forgiveness of sins, both came from the same power of right-standing with GOD.

Believers believe we can introduce someone to Jesus Christ for the forgiveness of their sins, but do Believers believe we can use the power of the Name of Jesus Christ and the urging of the Holy Spirit to speak healing for the body, deliverance from depression, or provision for acts of kindness? **Where is the logic?** What shall we do with the 23rd Psalm, "the Lord is my shepherd and **I shall not want," GOD has not changed,** and the promise of salvation is "*sozo* or total wellbeing" in the Greek. Jesus has sent the Holy Spirit, as part of Himself, to indwell Believers and to teach us about the gifts **Jesus finished at the cross.** In addition to the gifts Jesus provided, Believers have the authority GOD gave us at creation.

Do you know where trouble comes from?

John 10:10 The thief cometh not, but for to steal, and to kill, and to destroy I (Jesus) am come that they (Believers) might have life "*Zoe*", and that they might have it more abundantly.

If you believe, that Jesus' crucifixion and resurrection destroyed the power of Satan then Believers have power over the stealing, killing, and destroying of the devil.

The word for life in "abundant life", used here is zoe, zoie, (abundant life on earth) not eternal life (aionios zoie, eternal life) This scripture is **Not** merely to preserve but *impart* **LIFE** and communicate it in terms that are rich and exuberant. What a claim! What a Savior! Yet it is only a morsel or crumb of all the Lord's teaching; and Jesus, who said these words, must be either a liar or "the way, the truth, and the life" there can be no middle ground.

After reading John 10:10 is your mind, more consumed with the stealing, killing and destroying of the devil, or the more abundant life given by Jesus Christ? If your thinking is focused on the enemy and his lies, you may need to ponder and study what the abundant life of Jesus Christ means to you from the scriptures? The Lord's description of the victory over the enemy in our world is definitive as to "who does what to whom": it is the Believer's choice to believe in the victory or suffer the lies of the devil. After the Second World War, had ended, there was a

Japanese soldier in the Philippines who was the last living man in his company who lived in a cave for 35 years or so, killing people thinking the war was still active. Are you fighting any battles the Lord Jesus has won because you don't know the war is over? Remember, Almighty GOD won the war with the sin nature when Jesus was resurrected and restored to GOD's side. And the end of the war with sin was 1990 years ago and Believers inherited the victory.

The thief steals, kills, and destroys.

Jesus has brought "zoie" life with abundance.

The Church has not taught believers enough about the Holy Spirit and the power manifest with Holy Spirit inside you,

to do the works of GOD.

The Church needs to shout from the roof tops
that Jesus died to give
Believers the Holy Spirit
to be inside each Believer.

Without understanding the importance of a relationship with the Holy Spirit,

Believers are without mechanisms to dispel doubt
concerning the promises of GOD.
Doubt keeps miracles from happening
as a commonplace daily event.

Believers must act on the scriptures and **speak those things which be not as though they were.** Romans 4:17 **Again THINK ABOUT THIS: If you don't speak things as though they were, the way GOD designed, you will have things the way they are.** By speaking and believing you can exchange depression for peace and a heavy heart for joy.

Warning, We are entering a construction zone.
Foundation work ahead.

Questions;
>Did salvation come from the sinless Blood of our Savior?
>Where is the logic, for the "bread" in Communion?
>Is the bread, at remembrance of Jesus, for the total wellbeing of the Believer's life?

GOD did not allow His Son to be scourged, beaten, slapped, and humiliated without an important benefit to Believers. Sacrifices to GOD were always an animal without spot or blemish, Believers are new members of GOD's family. God's word says Jesus endured the **scourging as a gift for the Believers' healing** and that healing and deliverance is a part of Salvation.
>"Sozo" in the Greek language, is the word for total wellbeing.
>"Sozo" is used in the New Testament approximately 110 times 57 times meaning salvation and 53 times meaning total wellbeing, healed, or delivered.

Believers must believe in healing or *live with the consequence of unbelief* in the 39 stripes on the back of our Savior. The scourging and the promise derived from it, is not a relative truth. Listen to the Apostle Peter;
>1st Peter 2:23-4 Who, when he (Jesus) was reviled, reviled not again; when he (Jesus) suffered, he threatened not; but committed himself to him that judgeth righteously: Who his own self bare our sins in his own body on the tree, that we, being dead to sins, should live unto righteousness: **by whose stripes ye were healed (iaomai to make whole).**

Imagine the horrendous scourging of Jesus for Believer's health and total wellbeing. Imagine the body of the Lord broken for you and conceive, or picture in your mind, the love given in His sacrifice for you and store in your brain, the "thought picture" of your total wellbeing through the scourging of Jesus Christ and his love for you.

Do you believe the sinless blood was shed for Believer's salvation?

Do you believe the crushing of the Lord's body was for the Believer's total wellbeing?

Why did Jesus take the scourging and why did God allow it, if it had no purpose? **Where is the logic?** King Herod had Jesus scourged, in hopes, that the scourging would appease the Jews because he did not want to have the blood of Jesus on his hands, but **what was GOD's purpose?**

Imagine the Passion (love for Believers) of our Christ;

Imagine the scene of the scourging of Jesus Christ.

The 1st lash raised whelps and a few cuts.

The 2nd lash increased the cuts and added more whelps.

The 3rd lash increased the cuts and added more cuts.

The 4th lash added more cuts and exposed the nerves.

The 5th lash started peeling skin from the back, blood was everywhere.

The 6th lash started destroying the muscles of the back.

The 7th lash continued to destroy flesh and muscle.

The 8th lash continued to destroy flesh and muscle.

The 9th lash continued to destroy flesh and muscle.

The 10th lash continued to destroy flesh and muscle.

The 11th lash continued to destroy flesh and muscle.

The 12th lash continued to destroy flesh and muscle.

The 13th lash continued to destroy flesh and muscle.

The 14th lash continued to destroy flesh and muscle.

The 15th lash continued to destroy flesh and muscle.
The 16th lash continued to destroy flesh and muscle.
The 17th lash continued to destroy flesh and muscle.
The 18th lash continued to destroy flesh and muscle.
The 19th lash continued to destroy flesh and muscle.
The 20th lash continued to destroy flesh and muscle.
The 21st lash continued to destroy flesh and muscle.
The 22nd lash destroyed flesh, revealed bone. Blood
was everywhere
The 23rd lash destroyed flesh and revealed bone.
The 24th lash destroyed flesh and revealed bone.
The 25th lash destroyed flesh and revealed bone.
The 26th lash destroyed flesh and revealed bone.
The 27th lash destroyed flesh and revealed bone.
The 28th lash destroyed flesh and revealed bone.
The 29th lash destroyed flesh and revealed bone.
The 30th lash destroyed flesh and revealed bone.
The 31st lash began to reach organs and more nerves.
The 32nd lash began to rip at organs and nerves.
The 34th lash began to rip at organs and nerves.
The 35th lash began to rip at organs and nerves.
The 36th lash ripped at organs, bones, and nerves.
The 37th lash ripped at organs, bones, and nerves.
The 38th lash reached organs, bones, and nerves.
The 39th lash reached organs, bones, and nerves.

Why did God allow and why did Jesus take the scourging of the lashes? Jesus could have been stoned or speared. It was His sinless blood that produced our salvation. The Believer's redemption depended on the blood of Jesus, not the scourging. The scourging was so damaging and painful because it was for the healing of all flesh. **Now, that is some logic.**

The Passion of our Christ continues after the scourging:

Next promise fulfilled,

Jesus bore our sorrows and carried our grief on his shoulder as he carried the transom of the cross to the crucifixion location laboring up the hill until he received help from Simon, the Cyrene, a bystander. During the excruciating pain of the Crucifixion, our Savior suffered our griefs and sorrows, so we could exchange our griefs and sorrows for His love.

Jesus was pierced in the side for our transgressions and bruised for all Believer's iniquities,

Jesus was humiliated, mocked, and spat on, and punished to bring all Believes peace,

Jesus was made poor that Believers might become rich.

Isaiah 53, 2nd Corinthians 8:9, 2nd Peter 5:8

Logic says, Believers should have an irrevocable belief in the works of Jesus Christ and his gifts to Believers. **If you do not know** about the gifts given Believers or do not believe in healing and peace from Jesus, you will live without faith for the gifts GOD has given you?

Ask yourself," Why did Jesus take the scourging of the 39 lashes?" Where is the logic?
Jesus could have just pricked his little finger to deliver
his blood for all of mankind's sins,
why did he take the scourging?
and beatings?
and crown of thorns?
and the piercing of his side?
and the nails in his hands and feet?
He could have been stoned,
which was the normal execution by the Jewish people.

Believers inherited the finished works of Jesus Christ and the gift of the Holy Spirit and the Lord's authority to reign, in the abundant life. **If you believe.**

Believers saved and blessed with the Holy Spirit must spread the gospel of good news and tell all, the benefits of Salvation (sozo) to a dying world.

Listen to Jesus tell Believers about our destiny in the following scriptures;

> John 3:14 And as Moses lifted up the serpent in the wilderness, even so must the Son of man be lifted up: **That whosoever believeth in him should not perish but have eternal life.**
>
> Matthew 10:7 And proclaim as you go, saying, **'The kingdom of heaven is at hand.' Heal the sick, raise the dead, cleanse lepers, cast out demons.**
>
> Acts 1:8 But **you will receive power when the Holy Spirit has come upon you,** and you will be my witnesses in Jerusalem and in all Judea and Samaria, and to the end of the earth."
>
> John 14:12 **Verily, verily,** I say unto you, **He that believeth on me,** the works that I do shall he do also; and greater works than these shall he do; because I go unto my Father.
>
> Think about John 3:16 **"For God "so" loved** the world, that he gave his only Son, that **whoever believes** in him **should not perish** but have eternal life.

Any thought of your status, with GOD Almighty, that is less than total confidence in the perfectness of the sacrifice Jesus made for your complete redemption, health, freedom, love, including all benefits of being a child of God **is wrong.** Believers while on earth **should not perish,** defined as, Believers shall not diminish, be marred, lose, etc. And shall not perish is for Earth not Heaven. Certainly, there is no perishing in Heaven.

Study this next verse from the Apostle John and try to understand how you can be like **"Jesus is" in this world.**

> 1st John 4:16 And we have **known and believed the love** that God hath to us. **God is love;** and he that dwelleth in love dwelleth in God, and God in him. Herein is our love made perfect, that we may have boldness in the day of judgment: **because as he (Jesus) is, so are we in this world.**

Our Savior is (right now) as Believers are in this world, and we know that our Savior is redeemed, sanctified, healed, delivered, righteous, and perfect. **Believers must exchange how we see ourselves in the mirror (our body) for how GOD sees us (inside Believers in a Spiritual temple with our perfect Born-again Spirit).** We are children of Almighty GOD and the Holy Spirit is living inside Believers. Let the redeemed of the Lord, say so.

Let us take a minute to explore the construction of mankind. Mankind is 1% anything that dies and 99% anything that is eternal. The 1% is your body, eyes, ears, mouth, nose, hands, and brain and the 99% is the Believer's Spirit, soul, and mind.

Jesus, was not put to death,
but instead laid down his life and
committed His Spirit to GOD Almighty.

This is a Foundational principle of our faith; Jesus was not put to death. **He laid His life down,** because death had no power over Him, **He had power to pick up His life.** Listen to this scripture from Luke;

Luke 23:46 Then Jesus, calling out with a loud voice, said, **"Father, into your hands I commit my spirit!" And having said this he breathed his last.** Now when the centurion saw*(see note at chapter end) what had taken place, he praised God, saying, "Certainly this man was innocent!"

Jesus had no sin and therefore was not subject to death. Listen to the Apostle John;

John 10:17 Therefore doth my Father love me, because I lay down my life, that I might take it again. No man taketh it from me, but I lay it down of myself. **I have power to lay it down, and I have power to take it again.** This commandment have I received of my Father.

Believers also have the power to lay down your life when you are through with your purpose on earth. You do not have to be chased into death, of your body by the enemy. The Holy Spirit inside you is more powerful than the enemy of Believers and death has no power over you because there is no sin in your account.

Evaluating our belief in the Lord

If a Christian can only believe what they can see, hear, and touch; that Christian will not be able to believe the unseen world of the Spirit and will not communicate with the Holy Spirit living inside the Christian. Think about the following situations;

If you find yourself condemned in your heart for your actions, you are dealing with a **guilty conscience,** logic says, **you do not believe** that Jesus died for the sins of the world and there is now therefore **"no condemnation"** for those in Christ Jesus.

If you believe that any action, of any kind, or

elimination of any act will help a Christian obtain their salvation, **you have been misled.**

If you believe everything spiritual happens when you get to Heaven and you are just trying to get by until you die, **you have been deceived.**

If you come to church on Sunday so that you don't have to read your Bible, **you are a dummy and are missing GOD's love in your life.**

If you think or hope that being what you consider to be "good" will help God choose you, **you are mistaken.**

If you think you are OK because you know a lot of people at church that act worse than you; you are judgmental, prideful, and, **you can still go to "hell" because you may not be saved.**

Believer's actions motivated from pride or self-centeredness **stand in the way** of Believer's believing in God's complete forgiveness, healing, and confirmation of God's steadfast love. **Pride in what you have done, instead of thanksgiving for what GOD has created, is not "the truth" and will lead you to harden your heart and live without the benefits of your salvation.**

The Believer's daily life must be one of action, while resting in the guidance of the Holy Spirit because the mainstay of the New Covenant is the gift of the Holy Spirit to be in and on Believers for the power to reign in life.

If you are struggling; are you sure you have received the Holy Spirit?

If you are down, depressed, downtrodden, then you are not understanding what Christ has done for you at the Cross and you need the word of the Lord's peace and more promises to be planted in your heart, mind, and brain.

If you need healing, you need to hear the word of GOD on healing.

If you need provision, you need to hear the word of GOD on provision.

If you are depressed, you need to hear the word of GOD on peace.

If you feel unloved, you need to hear the word of GOD on GOD's love.

Remember GOD's name; "I am" the GOD of salvation, healing, provision, covering, and creation. Believers must cast your care on the cross because that is your inheritance, Jesus has taken everything that causes strife, for you, so that you might live in His love. You are an Ambassadorship of Jesus Christ to the world, are you ready to be confirmed and take your post?

Listen to these four Psalms about the power and peace from being led by the Spirit of GOD;

Psalms 19:7 The law of the LORD is **perfect,** reviving the soul; the testimony of the LORD is **sure,** making wise the simple;
the precepts of the LORD **are** right,
rejoicing the heart;
the commandment of the LORD
is **pure,**
enlightening the eyes;
the fear of the LORD is clean,
enduring forever;
the rules of the LORD are **true,** and
righteous altogether.
More to be **desired** are they than gold,
even much fine gold;
sweeter also than honey
and drippings of the honeycomb.
Moreover, by them is your servant warned;

in keeping them there is great reward.

Psalms 68:19 Blessed *be* the Lord, **who daily loadeth us** (Believers) ***with benefits***, even the God of our salvation. Selah. *He that is* our God *is* the God of salvation; and unto GOD the Lord *belong* the issues from death.

Bless the LORD, O my soul, and forget not **all his benefits:**
Who forgiveth all thine iniquities;
      Who healeth all thy diseases;
            Who redeemeth thy life
                from destruction;
                    Who crowneth thee
                with lovingkindness
         and tender mercies;
Who satisfieth thy mouth with good *things*;
so that thy youth is renewed like the eagle's.
        Psalms 103:2

      What shall I render unto the LORD for ***all his benefits*** toward me? I will take the cup of salvation and call upon the name of the LORD Psalms 116:12 I will offer to thee the sacrifice of thanksgiving, and will call upon the name of the LORD. Psalms 116:17

Conclusion; The two million plus Israelites were slaves in Egypt for over four hundred years and when GOD brought them out of Egypt **not one** was sick or feeble. The Israelis wandered in the desert for forty years and the scripture says they had food super naturally delivered every day, their clothes grew with them, their shoes did not wear out, there was cloud cover in the day-light and a cloud of light in the evening and night. If GOD did these miracles for the Israelis, are Believers to believe that GOD wants to live inside Believers in a disease-ridden body that is depressed, poor, and infested with demons? **The answer is no.**

The Spirit of the resurrected Jesus Christ,
in the person of the Holy Spirit is sent by GOD, the Father,

to all, who ask for the Holy Spirit,
            to live in a Temple not made with hands
                inside Believers
                        with the Believer's Born-again Spirit.

The question is; Do you believe GOD designed the crucifixion and resurrection for the saints to include salvation, sanctification, redemption and wisdom of the Lord given to Believers? If a Believer does not believe, in any and all of the gifts of GOD, **the Believer will have what you believe.**

Listen to the early church describe the state of affairs.
> Acts 4:29 And now, Lord, look upon their threats and grant to your servants to continue to speak your word with all boldness, **while you stretch out your hand to heal, and signs and wonders are performed through the name of your holy servant Jesus."** And when they had prayed, the place in which they were gathered together was shaken, and they were all filled with the Holy Spirit and continued to speak the word of God with boldness.

"What did the Centurion see that made him believe Jesus was the Son of GOD?" From his vantage point at the crucifixion, across the valley from the Temple, the Centurion could see the curtain in Temple rip from top to bottom, see the graves open in the cemetery, burial place in the valley, then the centurion was moved to guard the tomb to where he observed the resurrection.
The Centurion saw the earthquake and the rocks split,

- Curtain in the Temple ripped from top to bottom
- The graves open and the saints raised out of the graves with new bodies at the Lord's resurrection and the resurrected saints go into town and show themselves in the town.
- Sky turn black for 3 hours and turn to light as Jesus said, "it is finished".
- Saw the placing of the body in the tomb and the stone put in place and sealed and saw the empty tomb.
- Possibly saw the angels at the tomb who rolled away the stone.

When Jesus Christ was resurrected and went to Heaven, He delivered the First Fruits offering of the Resurrected saints, who were resurrected with Christ, and the Blood of the lamb slain from the foundation of time. He also sprinkled His blood where the expelled accuser, Satan, stood when he accused the saints in the Heavenly Temple of GOD. After the resurrection, Satan (accuser of the brethren) could no longer usurp the power of mankind that Adam and Eve gave to him in the Garden of Eden to be in the presence of Almighty GOD. Satan is but a shadow and without substance, he is a lie and the truth is not in him.

Listen and concentrate on each element of this scripture. This is one of the most important scriptures in the Bible.

One of the Most important scriptures in the Bible

Matthew 27:50   And Jesus cried out again with a loud voice and yielded up his spirit. And behold, the curtain of the temple was torn in two, from top to bottom. And the earth shook, and the rocks were split. **The tombs**

also were opened. And many bodies of the saints who had fallen asleep were raised, and coming out of the tombs after his resurrection they went into the holy city and appeared to many. When the centurion and those who were with him, keeping watch over Jesus, **saw the earthquake and what took place,** they were filled with awe and said, **"Truly this was the Son of God!"**

The graves were opened at the timing of the earthquake and three days later the Saints were resurrected as Christ was resurrected and went into the city and appeared to many in Jerusalem and then they went to Heaven with Jesus as part of the First Fruits offering to GOD Almighty of those to be resurrected and caught up at the next appearing of the Lord. (rapture) There are two elements to the First Fruits offering on the first day of the week at morning Prayers; one element is the wave offering of the harvest (resurrected saints) and the second element is the blood of a lamb without blemish. The Lord is the lamb without blemish and the resurrected saints are the blessed part of the soon coming rapture of the Church.

GOD's plan is marching forward.

> Revelation 12:10 And I heard a loud voice in heaven, saying, "Now the salvation and the power and the kingdom of our God and the authority of his Christ have come, **for the accuser of our brothers has been thrown down,** who accuses them day and night before our God. And they have conquered him by the blood of the Lamb and by the word of their testimony, for they loved not their lives even unto death.

Satan had access to Heaven because of the sin of Adam.

Jesus delivered his sinless blood and cast it in Heavenly places that needed cleansing from the accuser of the brethren. The devil no longer has access to GOD to accuse the brethren. Satan is now but a shadow.

CHAPTER 6

Control your thought life
or your thoughts will control you.

Salvation has been given, but not all are saved; healing has been
given, but not all are healed; deliverance from depression has
been given but not all are delivered; peace has been given. but
not all find their peace. Salvation, redemption, healing, peace,
and more are "Finished works of Jesus Christ ", **think about
this,** all of your sins were forgiven before you were even born,
because the universe of sin and the law, from which sin is judged,
was done away with "in total" at the cross. The sacrifice at the
cross was and is outside time; the cross is relevant for the
beginning of time, even before the flood, and relevant for today,
for your salvation. The redemption of the Lord is relevant for the
future; the sacrifice of Jesus is outside time, it is eternal; **when
you believe** you receive the eternal life given by Jesus Christ
given at His death at the cross. The eternal parts of the Believer
are with Christ at the right hand of GOD and on earth with the
Holy Spirit. This sounds crazy but it is logical; that if the
Believer's Spirit abides with God and GOD abides with Believers
there is a connection that is outside time, even right now: can you
see it with your mind.

The New Covenant is one of action by Believers.

The New Covenant "is" GOD inside Believers and sets up
Believers to act in concert with the Holy Spirit to reign in life

through action, with a heart of compassion.

Make a note; the phrases of the New Testament are all actions required from the Believers, not actions to ask GOD to do;

> "Cast your care", "be anxious for nothing", "speak to that mountain", present your bodies", "Pray unceasingly", "lay hands on the sick", "cast out devils", "take every thought captive", "ask, seek, knock", "praise Him", "put on the whole armor", "be strong", "draw near to GOD", resist the devil and he will flee", and more words of invisible action for Believers.

All of these phrases describe actions and yet Believers must rest in the control of the Holy Spirit instructions. The Holy Spirit will lead Believers to steward the estate of GOD and Jesus Christ for the benefit of others in the awesome authority GOD has given Believers.

Listen to Jesus in Matthew 6:20 speak about imagination, commitment, focus and direction;

> For where your treasure is, there your heart will be also. "The eye is the lamp of the body. **So, if your eye is healthy,** your whole body will be full of light, but if your eye is bad, your whole body will be full of darkness. If then the light in you is darkness, how great is the darkness! "No one can serve two masters, for either he will hate the one and love the other, or he will be devoted to the one and despise the other. **You cannot serve God and money.**

Do Not Be Anxious

> "Therefore, I tell you, **do not be anxious about your life,** what you will eat or what you will drink, nor about

your body, what you will put on. **Is not life more than food, and the body more than clothing?** Look at the birds of the air: they neither sow nor reap nor gather into barns, **and yet** your heavenly Father feeds them. Are you not of more value than they? And which of you by **being anxious** can add a single hour to his span of life? And why are you anxious about clothing? **Consider the lilies of the field, how they grow: they neither toil nor spin, yet I tell you, even Solomon (the richest man who has ever lived) in all his glory was not arrayed like one of these.** But if God so clothes the grass of the field, which today is alive and tomorrow is thrown into the oven, will he not much more clothe you, **O you of little faith**? Therefore **do not** be anxious, saying, 'What shall we eat?' or 'What shall we drink?' or 'What shall we wear?' For the Gentiles seek after all these things, and **your heavenly Father knows that you need them all.** But seek first the kingdom of God and his righteousness, and all these things will be added to you. **"Therefore do not be anxious about tomorrow,** for tomorrow will be anxious for itself. Sufficient for the day is its own trouble. Mathew 6:20-34

Therefore, **seek first the Kingdom of GOD, and His righteousness, and all the cares of the world will be fulfilled; because He is GOD Almighty and knows what you have need of today.** Can you separate yourself from the daily pursuit of money, to find the destiny of GOD for your life at your vocation? Imagine this; If GOD Almighty had a fireplace and a mantel your picture would be over the mantel, that is how much GOD cares for you.

What are Believers to do
When sickness, depression,
Or lack is found in a Believer?

First, not all sickness and depression are from the curses of the law but can be from consequences of man-made decisions; for example; overeating until you cause yourself heart problems, depression from your fatness and knee problems from your weight are not a curse. **Consequences of man-made decisions to operate in your own power and not operate in GOD's word will have man-made consequences. Maladies originating from consequences require a miracle instead of faith in the Lord's sacrifice for your healing.** The Believer can turn around most consequences of man-made misguided actions by learning to capture thoughts for the ill-fated consequence like overeating. Certainly, the Bible instructs Believers to do everything in moderation and not to be a glutton.

Believers, who are suffering from sickness and other curses, that Believers were redeemed from at the cross; are fighting a battle with faith, unbelief, and doubt, which will block a divine outcome. Doubt or unbelief stifles GOD's grace. Believers must dominate doubt, or you will live without the grace, GOD has for you. **For action against doubt, Believers must reassure our hearts with the word of GOD. Do not allow** a negative emotion or circumstance to have a negative response from the Believer. A Believer's emotion are not just something that happens, you are a free moral agent and you are in charge of your feelings. GOD has given you authority to respond with joy and gladness in the midst of a negative situation. Remember the words of Jesus when He said, "Let not your heart be troubled neither let it be afraid." It is in your authority to let not your heart be troubled and neither be afraid. (John 14:27)
      This is a time to understand more about the Believer's

brain; When you exchange your sin nature for GOD's loving nature, the foundation of your brain operates from a positive motivation from the love of GOD. This foundation of love does not allow a negative thought to remain unless the mind continues to nurture the negative thought until it is more powerful than the peace from GOD's word you have stored in your brain for the mind to control the chaotic thought.

What happens if you do not control your thoughts?
A brain operating on self-centered motivation is always on edge because fear is resident in self-centered thinking. The self-centered brain acts as their own god and therefore the mind has no mechanism to cast fear and anxiety on the Promises of God. When the mind allows thoughts of stress and anxiety, you are allowing chaos in your brain and all of the stress related diseases are at work in your body because your brain is not able to rest. Destructive thoughts grow and develop energy and that energy causes more chaos.

How do you get rid of bad thoughts and fears?
Think about your thoughts; Has your focus on GOD dimmed, what is capturing the majority of your time? Detoxing your brain by the introduction of scripture will override thoughts of doubt and your brain will return to operating in GOD's rest. To regain control of your thoughts and the actions of your brain you must focus on GOD's love by introducing scripture and meditating on your identity in Jesus Christ to restore the Lord's peace to your mind.

For example; Believers own the fruit of the Spirit, the fruit came packed inside your new Creation Spirit. The Believer when confronted with anxiety can exchange anxiety for the peace of GOD by calling on the brain mindset of peace, the peace is yours Jesus Christ gave it to you. "Let not your heart be troubled neither let it be afraid" John 14:27 If **you** don't capture chaotic thoughts, they will cause chaos in your brain.

Again, the command is for the Believer to NOT LET YOUR HEART be troubled neither let it be afraid. The Believer's thought life is in the Believer's control.

2nd Timothy 3:15 and how from childhood you have been acquainted with the sacred scriptures, which are able to make you wise for salvation through faith in Christ Jesus. **All Scripture is breathed out by God and profitable for teaching, for reproof, for correction, and for training in righteousness, that the man of God may be complete, equipped for every good work.**

The Believers heart needs to have an image of GOD's supernatural love for you, in your Spirit and mind from which all motivation springs forth. The New Covenant or Post-Cross life of the Believer is powerful to the bringing down of strongholds (chaotic mindsets) by choosing the thoughts to retain in your heart and mind; you do not have to remain anxious when you have the power to exchange chaotic thoughts for peace (Shalom- peace; total wellbeing) from Jesus Christ. **Remember you control your thoughts and there is no fear in love. (1st John 4:18)**

Let not your heart be troubled by:
The Devil, unbelief,
riches, stupidity, persecution,
or situations that offer a choice to doubt.

There are five main areas to overcome;

Christians operating without wisdom or consultation

with the Holy Spirit before acting, will act without supply from GOD's grace.

Christians leaning on their own understanding, when GOD is inside you for consultation and leadership, will have a man-made outcome.

Persecution for faith in GOD for being an Ambassador for Jesus Christ is judgment against the Lord not you, do not receive condemnation.

Riches and seeking for riches mask the Believers need for GOD and lead to pride in the Believer's accomplishments.

Not discerning the Lord's body of sacrifice in remembrance of our Lord, especially during the breaking of bread and drinking the cup has consequences.

Believing Christians, not knowing better than to live under the curses when Believers have been redeemed.

Explore the following scriptures for the direction from GOD's word.

If a Believer desires a divine outcome, the Believer must request and receive the leading of the Holy Spirit "first"; as you make decisions for your day, casting your care on Him who cares for you, speaking to the Holy Spirit for direction (before acting to start your day) and remaining in the power of your relationship with GOD. **Believers have been given standing in this world to use the Name of Jesus for power to change the world with the invisible power of faith and the gift of grace from GOD. When you speak life to a situation in the name of Jesus, the power of GOD is at hand to supply anything necessary for good works of kindness.**

Believers will only find yourself in the ditch, when you act and do not have a confirmation of your daily plan, from the Holy Spirit. Remember; If GOD had a wallet, your picture would be in GOD's wallet, do you have a picture of GOD in your wallet (heart). Don't relate to Almighty GOD relate to Abba Father or Daddy GOD, you have been adopted into His family. Can you relate to this truth for your life? Listen to this scripture declaring that Believers have the mind of Christ.

> 1st Corinthians 2:14 The natural person does not accept the things of the Spirit of God, for they are folly to him, and he is not able to understand them because they are **spiritually discerned.** The spiritual person judges all things, but is himself to be judged by no one. "For who has understood the mind of the Lord so as to instruct him?" **But we (Believers) have the mind of Christ**.

Believers are **not** restricted to your mind, you have the luxury to call on the "mind of Christ", think about this statement, "if you do not cast your care on Jesus, you will still have your care". Care and anxiety are **not** from the Lord and is the opposite of peace and is the image of fear. Care, anxiety, fear, and unbelief are the foundation for all the negative images in your life and these issues come out of a heart that has been infected with doubt. A Believer's man-made actions will have consequences and the Believer's spirit filled actions will have divine outcomes. The Believer must STOP idle words and bring every thought captive to the word of GOD in your heart and run your proposed actions by the Holy Spirit for approval. **Remember,** your brain cannot function correctly when thoughts of anxiety and stress, are causing chaos to the functions of your mind and brain, therefore cast out the doubt in our heart, knowing you have the Spirit of GOD, inside you, for comfort, revelation, and to tell the Believer things to come. If a Believer never ask the Holy Spirit, "what is to come?" the Holy Spirit will not have the opportunity to tell the

Believer, "things to come" because you are a free will Believer and every choice is yours to make.

Listen to the Apostle Paul describe the awesome power of being a Believer and importance of maintaining your mind and thoughts to reassure your heart of who you are and whose you are;

God's Everlasting Love

Romans 8:31 So what should we say about this?

If God is for us, no one can stand against us.

And God is with us.

He even let his own Son suffer for us.

God gave his Son for all of us.

So now with Jesus,

God will surely give us all things.

Who can accuse the people God has chosen?

No one!

God is the one who makes them right.

Who can say that God's people are guilty?

No one! Christ Jesus died for us,

but that is not all.

He was also raised from death.

And now he is at God's right side,

speaking to him for us.

Can anything separate us from Christ's love?

Can trouble or problems or persecution

separate us from his love?

If we have no food or clothes

or face danger or even death,

will that separate us from his love?

The answer is no.

The word of this scripture is your response

to anxiety, strife, fear, and unbelief.

This scripture is so strong, "If GOD is for us, no one can stand against us." And this scripture is the Believer's response to anxiety, strife, fear, and unbelief. The image in the Believer's heart when confronted with, "the thief cometh", **stop,** visualize the direction you are going, evaluate and then let the good Shepherd lead you through His Spirit **shouting GOD is with me and no person or thing can stand against me, I am the righteousness of GOD in Christ Jesus.**

The victory has been won, but the enemy is fighting to undermine your remembrance of the victory and your relationship with your GOD. Consider the next four scriptures (below) that form the foundation for evaluating the causes for negative life situations. "Who did what to whom?" or "Why do bad things happen to good people?". How do Believers identify the cause behind negative situations in a Believer's daily life?

The following scriptures identify the Lords delivery of the victory over the Devil, victory over fear, victory over the drive for riches, and identify losing focus of the Lord's body during the drinking of the cup and the breaking of the bread.

The Devil;

> John 10:10 The thief cometh not, but for **to steal, and to kill, and to destroy:** I (Jesus) am come that they **might have life, and that they might have *it* more abundantly.**

Fear;

> 2nd Timothy 1:7 For God hath **not given** us the spirit of fear; but of **power,** and of **love,** and of a **sound mind.** There is no fear in love. Perfect love cast our all fear. 1st John 4:18

Search for riches;

> 1st Timothy 6:9-10 But they that **will be rich** fall into

temptation and a snare, and into many foolish and hurtful lusts, which drown men in destruction and perdition. For the love of money is the root of all evil: which while some coveted after, they have erred from the faith, and pierced themselves through with many sorrows.

Not remembering your Savior and His sacrifice of love;

1st Corinthians 11:28 Let a person examine himself, then, and so eat of the bread and drink of the cup. For anyone who eats and drinks **without discerning the body (Jesus Christ) eats and drinks judgment on himself.** That is why many of you are **weak and ill, and some have died.**

The abundant life is available to those who act on and rest in the leadership of the Holy Spirit and authority given Believers by GOD. When Believers understand and have a visual understanding of the cause of the problems confronting Believers, they can summon the appropriate word of GOD from there heart to address all problems with a spiritual solution. The outcome of the attacks of the devil, problems of being self-centered, constant search for riches, and **not** honoring GOD for who GOD is and what GOD has done can be countered with the **"Victory of Jesus",** over any and all negative situations.

The Believer can live the abundant life through the Lord's victory and resting in the wisdom of the Holy Spirit, committed to the word of the Lord, communicating with the Holy Spirit, with action guided by love in the Believer's heart. It is not sound doctrine to believe "all things work together for good" and contradict the explanation of the scriptures above as to why negative situations happen to good people.

Believers have inherited victory.
Do you have an image of the inheritance?

The scriptures above allow a Believer to evaluate their position with regard to the actions of the devil and his influence on the human mindset. The constant question for Believers to answer; is your "present situation" part of the abundant life? The choice for Believers is living from the "Victory of Jesus" or living subject to outside forces? The devil is constantly buffeting and trying to influence Believers **to create fear, anxiety, and unbelief and bring chaos to your brain.**

> If the Believer does not capture the thoughts of doubt, questioning your righteousness, the Believer's faith will turn to fear.

To live "from the Victory" of Jesus over; the power of Satan, the curses of the law, death, Hell, and the grave, a Believer **must believe and not doubt.** Do not think, you are going to win a victory **for Jesus Christ, He is the one who overcame the world, it is His victory, and the Believer must find the way into the Lord's victory, not one of your own.**

Consider this: A Believer can only act on, what they know about GOD. **Believers have inherited the Lord's victory; to be successful in having faith for the promises of GOD, a Believer must know what the promises are;**

> The GOD inside Believers knows what you have need for today.
> The GOD inside Believers is your wisdom.
> The GOD inside Believers is your peace.
> The GOD inside Believers is your healer.
> The GOD inside Believers is your resurrection and life.
> The GOD inside Believers has brought you the fruit of the Spirit available for your use right now.

Now that Believers are or can be filled with the Holy Spirit; it is the responsibility of the Believer to act with the power and authority of GOD's promises to do the works of GOD and guard your heart and brain. The Believer is ready and able to bring forth the will of GOD by acting on the word of GOD, in concert with the Holy Spirit, for themselves and others.

Paint this picture in your mind, the inheritance of the Saints;
> The Lord's blood redeemed the Believer's sin, His stripes healed our diseases, on His shoulders He bore our sorrows and carried our griefs, He was pierced for our transgressions, His body was   bruised for our iniquities, He was punished to bring us peace, and He was made poor that we might become rich. Isaiah 53 and 2nd Corinthians

Constantly remember; you are GOD's representative and ambassador on earth and God did not appoint you ambassador without giving you the authority and power to do the job.
> 2nd Corinthians 5:19 To wit, that God was in Christ, reconciling the world unto himself, not imputing their trespasses unto them; and hath committed unto us the word of reconciliation. Now then we are ambassadors for Christ

Believers need to read your employment agreement (Bible) to understand your authority in Christ Jesus through the Holy Spirit inside you. Do you remember the old story of the man, whose job it was to drain the swamp but was continuously distracted by the alligators snapping at his back-side. The devil is the alligators in that story, and it is the Believers job to stay focused on being an Ambassador for Jesus Christ. Listen to the ways the devil works to distract Believers;

**Again, what do Believers do, when their life
is plagued with fear anxiety and lack?**

GOD has given everyone in the world the dignity of choice to follow Him or a god of your choice. The devil **cannot** take **the peace** you have been given by Jesus Christ, **the Believer** must give his peace away by accepting the fear thoughts from the enemy and not knowing about or not using the power of GOD and the authority of the Believer to squash the opportunity to fear.

The Devil **cannot** take **the health** of a Believer given by the stripes suffered by Jesus Christ, the Believer must give their health away by doubting GOD's word on healing and/or squander their health with bad habits, which is in opposition to GOD's word.

The **thoughts** of a Believer NOT brought to the Lordship of Jesus, result in the Believer believing the lie of the devil and following the enemies leading, denying the Believer's authority to capture every thought and live in victory.

The **curses of the law** are not part of the New Covenant life, if the Believer knows and understands the inheritance, the Believer has received from Jesus Christ. Believers do not have to live in the curses of the law, you have been redeemed from the curses of the law. The redemption for the curses has been "Paid for in full", only the blessings remain in effect. If you believe and not doubt.

Sickness and depression and poverty are part of the curse and **Jesus redeemed Believers from the curse.** Listen to the curses:
Deuteronomy 28:16 Cursed shall you be in the city and cursed shall you be in the field. Cursed shall be your

basket and your kneading bowl. Cursed shall be the fruit of your womb and the fruit of your ground, the increase of your herds and the young of your flock. Cursed shall you be when you come in and cursed shall you be when you go out. "The LORD will send on you curses, confusion, and frustration in all that you undertake to do, until you are destroyed and perish quickly on account of the evil of your deeds, because you have forsaken me. The LORD will make the pestilence stick to you until he has consumed you off the land that you are entering to take possession of it. The LORD will strike you with wasting disease and with fever, inflammation and fiery heat, and with drought and with blight and with mildew. They shall pursue you until **you perish.**

Do not give away the victory and "perish", Jesus died to give you "the abundant life" and Believers "shall not Perish". Constantly create an image of yourself with Jesus at the right hand of GOD and the Holy Spirit inside you with your born-again spirit. All through your day say, **"I am the righteousness of GOD in Jesus Christ".** Say it often, it is the TRUTH. Stop and say it right now. "I am in right-standing with GOD" in Christ Jesus.

Galatians 3:13 The law says we are under a curse for not always obeying it. But Christ took away that curse. He changed places with us and put himself under that curse. The Scriptures say, "Anyone who is hung on a tree is under a curse." **Because of what Jesus Christ did, the blessing God promised to Abraham was given to all people.** Christ died so that by believing in him we could have the (Holy) Spirit that God promised and the blessings of Abraham.

Listen to the blessings that remain.

Deuteronomy 28:2 If you will obey the LORD your God, all these blessings will come to you and be yours: He will bless you in the city and in the field. He will bless you and give you many children. He will bless your land and give you good crops. He will bless your animals and let them have many babies. He will bless you with calves and lamb's. He will bless your baskets and pans and fill them with food. He will bless you at all times in everything you do. And there are many more blessings.

These blessings are yours, if you are a Believer, but they are over 1990 years old and other blessings are older. These blessings are the inheritance of Believers in Jesus Christ, who believing them by faith speak the blessings, bringing them to life in the present.

Believers must, seek first the Kingdom of GOD and His righteousness or they are fools. These are not my words but those of our GOD, listen as we read the first Proverb.

The Call of Wisdom

Can you imagine; The creator of all wisdom is abiding in Believers, in fact the Temple of GOD is inside Believers? Listen to this description of wisdom; In this Proverb, the Holy Spirit can be substituted for the word wisdom.

Proverbs 1:20 **Listen! Wisdom is shouting in the streets.** She is crying out in the marketplace. She (wisdom) is calling out where the noisy crowd gathers: "Fools, how long will you love being ignorant? How long will you make fun of wisdom? How long will you hate knowledge? I wanted to tell you everything I knew and give you all my knowledge, but you didn't listen to my advice and teaching.

"I tried to help, but you refused to listen. I offered my

hand, but you turned away from me. You ignored my advice and refused to be corrected. So I will laugh at your troubles and make fun of you when **what you fear happens.** Disasters will strike you like a storm. Problems will pound you like a strong wind. Trouble and misery will weigh you down. "Fools will call for me, but I will not answer. They will look for me, but they will not find me. **That is because they hated knowledge.** They refused to fear and respect the LORD. They ignored my advice and refused to be corrected. **They filled their lives with what they wanted. They went their own way, so they will get what they deserve.**

"Fools die because they refuse to follow wisdom. They are content to follow their foolish ways, and that will destroy them. **But those who listen to me will live in safety and comfort. They will have nothing to fear."**

Notice; Fools die because they refuse to follow wisdom (GOD). The word wisdom is a picture of GOD. Everyday should begin with the Believer and the Holy Spirit meeting to get consensus for the plan of the day. Plans, that do not include wisdom of GOD **will not** have the supply for the needs of the plan and will not result in a divine outcome. **Fear is faith in evil and peace is faith in GOD,** those who listen and follow the Holy Spirit will live in peace, provision, safety, and comfort. This Proverb is an old Testament passage but in the New Covenant life the Holy Spirit can be substituted for wisdom in this passage and it is relevant to Believers for today.

Listen to yet another proverb: A relationship with GOD demands following GOD with the Believer's plans and goals. To follow GOD, **you must be going in the same direction.**

**Trust in the Lord, through the Holy Spirit,
with All Your Heart and
Lean not to your own understanding,
Ask GOD before planning your day
for His guidance.**

Proverbs 3:1-12 My son, do not forget my teaching, but let your heart keep my commandments, **for length of days and years of life and peace they will add to you.** Let not steadfast love and faithfulness (GOD) forsake you; bind them around your neck; **write them on the tablet of your heart. So you will find favor and good success in the sight of God and man.**
Trust in the LORD with all your heart, and do not lean on your own understanding. **In all your ways acknowledge him, and he will make straight your paths.** Be not wise in your own eyes; fear the LORD, and turn away from evil. **It will be healing to your flesh and refreshment to your bones.**
Honor the LORD with your wealth and with the first fruits of all your produce; then your barns will be filled with plenty, and your vats will be bursting with wine.
My son, do not despise the LORD's discipline or be weary of his reproof, for the LORD reproves him whom he loves, as a father the son in whom he delights.

The Proverbs are full of wisdom that lead to a life of fulfillment, happiness, and keep chaos from your brain allowing Believers to stay in the Lord's rest.

THE END

Also by the Author

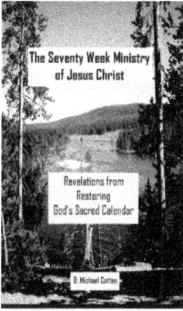

The Seventy Week Ministry of Jesus
Christ: Revelations from Restoring
God's Sacred Calendar
by Michael Cotten
ISBN: 978-0982480274
260 pages, $15.99

You're Not Special Because You Love
God . . . You're Special Because God
Loves You!
by Michael Cotten
ISBN: 978-1936497034
110 pages, $14.99

The Passtion of the Christ: As It Really
Happened
by Michael Cotten
ISBN: 978-1-936497-19-5
197 pages, $16.99

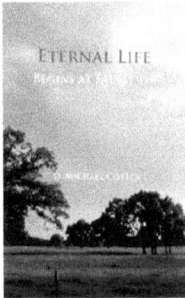

Eternal Life Begins at Salvation
by Michael Cotten
ISBN# 978-1-936497-25-6
101 pages, $14.99

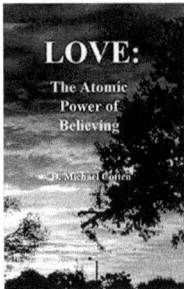

Love: the Atomic Power of God
by Michael Cotten
ISBN# 978-1-936497-33-1
115 pages, $14.99

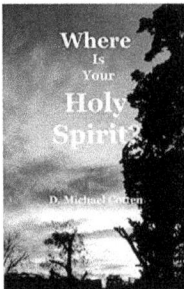

Where Is Your Holy Spirit
by Michael Sotten
ISBN#: 978-1936497379
156 pages, $16.99

Searchlight Press
Who are you looking for?
Publishers of thoughtful Christian books since 1994.
PO Box 554
Henderson, TX 75653-0554
214.662.5494
info@Searchlight-Press.com
www.Searchlight-Press.com

www.ingramcontent.com/pod-product-compliance
Lightning Source LLC
Chambersburg PA
CBHW071443090426
42737CB00011B/1764